IN NO TIME

Word
2000

IN NO TIME

Rainer Walter Schwabe

Prentice
Hall

AN IMPRINT OF PEARSON EDUCATION

PEARSON EDUCATION LIMITED

Head Office:
Edinburgh Gate
Harlow CM20 2JE
Tel: +44 (0)1279 623623
Fax: +44 (0)1279 431059

Head Office:
128 Long Acre
London WC2E 9AN
Tel: +44 (0)207 447 2000
Fax: +44 (0)207 240 5771

First published in Great Britain 2000
© Pearson Education Limited 2000

First published in 1990 as *Word 2000: leicht, klar, sofort*
by Markt & Technik Buch- und Software-Verlag GmbH
Martin-Kollar-Straße 10–12
D-81829 Munich
GERMANY

Library of Congress Cataloging in Publication Data
Available from the publisher.

British Library Cataloguing in Publication Data
A CIP catalogue record for this book can be obtained from the British Library.

ISBN 0-13-025785-0

10   9   8   7   6   5   4   3   2   1

Translated and typeset by Cybertechnics, Sheffield.
Printed and bound in Great Britain by Henry Ling Ltd at The Dorset Press, Dorchester, Dorset.

The publishers' policy is to use paper manufactured from sustainable forests.

Contents

Dear reader   1

The keyboard   2

The mouse   6

The first steps   8

Starting Word 10
The Assistant – 'with a little help
    from my friend' 11
Choosing an Assistant 12
Exiting Word 15

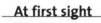

At first sight   18

The structure of Word 20
Activating and deactivating toolbars 24
ScreenTips for beginners 27
Formatting marks 29
The Zoom function 32
Take a break or go on to the next chapter? 34

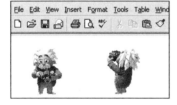

Forget Tipp-Ex! No more mistakes   36

Correcting mistakes via the keyboard 38
The Word spelling checker 40
Practise, practise ... and practise again! 44
Take a break or go on to the next chapter? 46

4 Formatting text 48

Formatting text 50
Other formatting options 53
Formatting via the keyboard 55
Fonts: types and sizes 56
Removing formatting 58
Aligning text 59
Line spacing 60

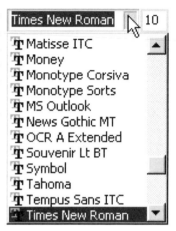

5 Saving and printing 62

Saving text 64
Saving changes 69
Save or Save As...? 70
Saving to diskette 72
Print Preview 75
Printing a document 76
The 'Full Screen' view 78

Dear Ms Brown

My wife and I have set up a new boutique at 44 '
invite you to the launch of our new collection at

Yours sincerely

6 Accessing, saving and deleting documents 80

Accessing documents 82
Protecting data from unauthorised access 87
Deleting documents 92
Practise, practise ... and practise again! 95

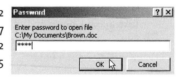

7 Writing your first letter — 98

Creating lists 100
Moving and copying text 103
The Thesaurus 106
Finding and replacing text 111
The 'Format Painter' button 114
Practise, practise ... and practise again! 116

8 The perfect letter: templates and wizards — 120

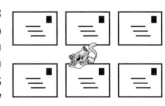

Headers and footers 122
Different views 125
Inserting a text box 126
Inserting the current date 135
Saving templates 139
Opening templates 141
Templates in Word 142
The Wizards 144

9 One letter – several addressees — 146

What is Mail Merge? 148
Creating a form letter 149
The data source 151
Field names 151
Saving data sources 155
Editing data sources 157
Inserting merge fields 160
The salutation 164
If ... then ... else 165
Merging a data source with
  a form letter 170
Practise, practise ... and practise again! 173

10 Stop – no more repetition   174

AutoComplete 176
AutoText and AutoCorrect? 179
Creating AutoText 179
Inserting AutoText 181
AutoCorrect 183
Using AutoText, AutoCorrect and
   tips in letters.. 185
Practise, practise ... and practise again! 189

11 Cards, fun and pictures with Word   190

Inserting ClipArt pictures 192
Editing pictures 196
The drawing toolbar 202
Casting a shadow 205
WordArt – special text effects 206
Text in pictures 209
Talking pictures 213

12 Keeping track of addresses, birthdays ...   218

Inserting tables 220
Table headings.. 221
Inserting symbols 222
Specifying a table heading 225
Entering text into tables 226
Selecting cells 228
Inserting rows 232
Inserting columns 233
Changing column width 234
Sorting in tables 237
Tables and borders 239
AutoFormat 241
Tables with tabs 242
Practise, practise ... and practise again! 250

13 Customising Word 254

Integrating buttons 256
Creating menu options 266
Defining your own keyboard shortcuts 270
Practise, practise ... and practise again! 277

14 Marginal notes: footnotes and page numbers 280

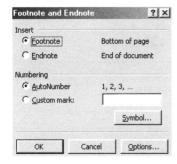

Inserting footnotes 282
Editing footnotes 286
Inserting page numbers 293
Practise, practise ... and practise again! 296

15 Help options 298

The Assistant – with a little help
    from a friend 299
What's This? 305

Appendix   308

Solutions 308
Quick text selection with the mouse 310
Keyboard shortcuts 315
What are all those keys for? 323
Getting to grips with Word 328

Glossary   343

Index   364

Dear reader

Never forget that mighty oaks from tiny acorns grow. Let's start at the beginning by asking the question 'What is Word?'

With the help of numerous examples this book will acquaint you step by step with Word.

My personal aim is to help you to get over the initial inhibitions which are always experienced by beginners embarking on something new.

The chapters are designed to be useful in practice, too.

I would advise you to have a go at the tasks. They not only reinforce your knowledge, but also outline new paths.

Finally, I would like to thank all participants of my introductory courses to Word. They have not only shown me which problems are experienced by beginners, but also inspired me to write this book. My particular thanks to those participants who 'didn't know the first thing' about Windows when they started, who thought a mouse was vermin, and who, as the course progressed, really got into Word.

I am sure you will become just as enthusiastic about Word as my 'guinea pigs'. That is why after reading the book you, too, will be able to say: 'Word – I learnt it IN NO TIME!'

Incidentally, if you like it and you want to learn Excel, have a look at Excel IN NO TIME.

Rainer Walter Schwabe

The following three pages show you how your computer keyboard is structured. Groups of keys are dealt with one by one to make it easier to understand.
Most of the computer keys are operated exactly like keys on a typewriter.
However, there are a few additional keys which are designed specifically for computer work.
See for yourself ......

Typewriter keys

Use these keys exactly as you do on a typewriter.
The Enter key is also used to send commands to your computer.

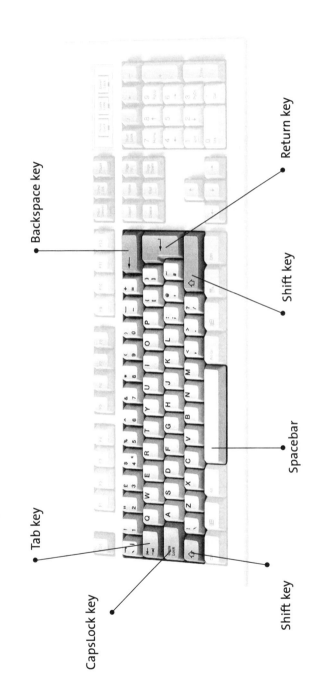

Tab key

CapsLock key

Backspace key

Shift key

Spacebar

Shift key

Return key

Special keys, function keys, status lights, numeric key pad

Special keys and function keys are used for special tasks in computer operation. Ctrl -, Alt - and AltGr keys are usually used in combination with other keys. The Esc key can cancel commands, while Insert and Delete can be used, amongst other things, to insert and delete text.

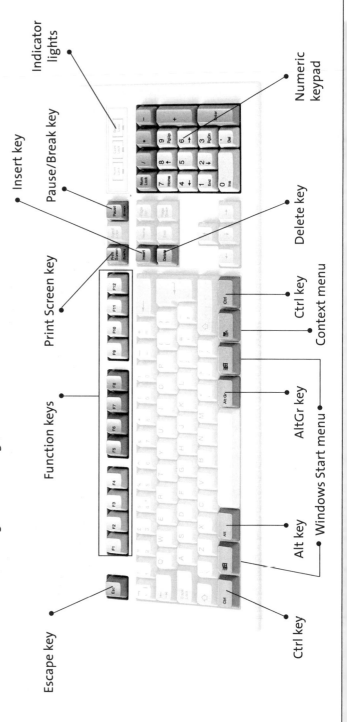

Escape key

Ctrl key

Alt key

Windows Start menu

Function keys

Print Screen key

AltGr key

Context menu

Insert key

Pause/Break key

Indicator lights

Numeric keypad

Delete key

Ctrl key

Navigation keys

These keys are used to move around the screen.

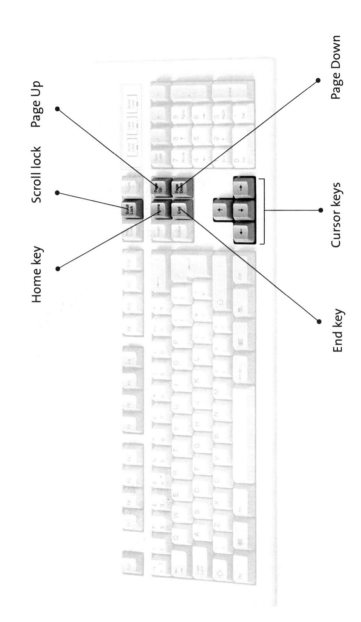

Scroll lock   Page Up

Home key

Page Down

Cursor keys

End key

'Click on ...'

means: press once briefly on a button.

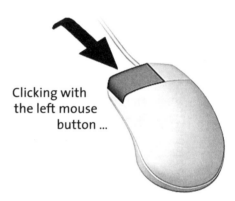

Clicking with
the left mouse
button ...

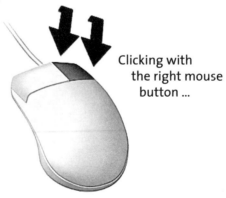

Clicking with
the right mouse
button ...

'Double-click on ...'

means: press the left button
twice briefly in quick
succession

Double-clicking

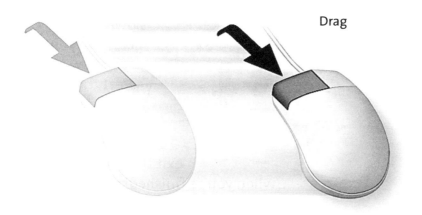

'Drag ...'

means: click on an object with the left
mouse button, keep the button
pressed, move the mouse to drag
the item to another position.

Drag

7

What's in this chapter:

There is a first time for everything in life: the first baby steps, the first day at school, the first best friend, the first kiss, the first disappointment ... and the first time you work with Word! Just as every experienced driver has to learn to drive, a beginner has to take his first steps in Word. Sit down behind the steering wheel and set off slowly in first gear: you will learn how to start the software in different ways and how to exit the program when you're finished!

You are going to learn about:

Starting Word   10
The Assistant – 'with a little help
  from my friend'   11
Choosing an Assistant   12
Exiting Word   15

Starting Word

Before you write any text in Word, you need to launch the program. This is one of the easiest ways – Word 2000 is a **program.** As with launching most programs, you click on the Windows **Start** button which is located in the bottom left hand corner of your screen.

In the **Start** menu, **Word** is automatically created as a separate item after successful installation. This is where you start the software on your screen.

The procedures outlined in the following steps are the same as for starting various other programs such as Excel, PowerPoint, Outlook or Access.

1 Click on the START button. The **Start menu** appears.

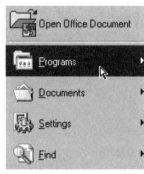

2 Select the PROGRAMS item.

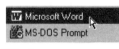

3 Windows opens an additional window, which is called a **submenu.** Select MICROSOFT WORD: the program starts.

After start-up the **user interface** of Word 2000 appears.

A **user interface** is the whole image of a program you see on the screen.

The Assistant – 'with a little help from my friend'

One additional feature of Word is the amusing animations available to you. At the first start-up of the software a bubbly **Assistant** immediately appears on the screen. Here it is a paper clip. It will help you to use the software.

How to hide the Assistant

The Assistant can be very helpful. You may choose to work with it, but you do not have to. To hide the Assistant:

Point the mouse at the Assistant.

Hide

Options...
Choose Assistant...
Animate!

Press the right mouse button.

Select HIDE ASSISTANT.

The 'little helper' disappears from screen.

How to activate the Assistant

In this book you will work with the Assistant, so you can activate him again.

Click on the ? button.

The Assistant reappears.

Choosing an Assistant

Word offers you a choice of Assistants. Which one you choose is a matter of taste. When you click on CHOOSE ASSISTANT, a selection of helpers appears.

1 Point the mouse at the Assistant.

2 Press the right mouse button.

3 Click on CHOOSE ASSISTANT.

You are spoiled for choice. Should you decide to change your **Assistant**, you will need to insert the **Office 2000 installation CD**. Confirm the selected assistant with *OK* (more information about the Assistants can be found in Chapter 15 'Help options').

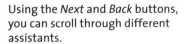

TIP

Using the *Next* and *Back* buttons, you can scroll through different assistants.

Click on *Next*.

Choose an Assistant.
Confirm with the *OK* button.

⚠ **Microsoft Word**

The selected Assistant character is not available.
This feature is not currently installed. Would you like to install it now?

Yes   No

If necessary insert the Office 2000 installation CD, and select *Yes*.

Exiting Word

After having started Word, try closing the program again in order to acquaint yourself with the first steps. Use the **Menu bar** for this.

In the **Menu bar**, you can call up commands such as EXIT or PRINT by opening the appropriate menu with the left mouse button and then selecting (clicking on) the appropriate item in the open menu.

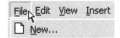

Click on the FILE menu option.

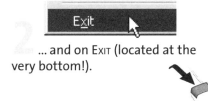

... and on EXIT (located at the very bottom!).

If Word asks you this question (it may not!), simply click on *No* with the left mouse button.

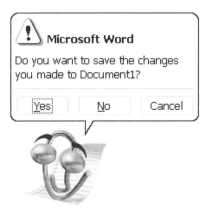

Alternative ways of exiting Word

There are two further options: you can exit Word directly by **double-clicking** on the **Word symbol** (top left) or by clicking on the **cross (X)** top left **once** with the left mouse button.

Double click with the
left mouse button

Simple click with the
left mouse button

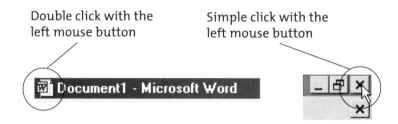

Now you are probably thinking that, so far, you have not done anything with Word! You have learnt – just like in your first driving lesson – how to start and switch off the motor. Well, let's start the motor – oh, sorry – the program and open the book at Chapter 2 'At first sight'. You are setting off in first gear.

2

What's in this chapter:

Start Word and you can see a completely unknown world on your screen, a world which is as alien to you as earth was to ET or Mars to NASA, a world you want to explore. How is Word structured and what is the significance of all of those buttons and grey surfaces?

You already know about:

Starting Word   10
The Assistant – 'with a little help from my friend'   11
Choosing an Assistant   12
Exiting Word   15

You are going to learn about:

The structure of Word   20
Activating and
    deactivating toolbars   24
ScreenTips for beginners   27
Formatting marks   29
The Zoom function   32

The structure of Word

Menu bar

File Edit View Insert Format Tools Table Window Help

Normal — Times New Roman — 10 — **B** *I* U

Standard toolbar   Formatting toolbar

Once you have launched the program you will see the user interface of Word 2000. At the very top there is the **command area** (menu bar, standard and formatting toolbars). Here, as indicated by the name, commands are called up and executed via the **mouse** or the **keyboard**.

Tools Table Window Help

ABC Spelling and Grammar... F7

1

In the TOOLS menu, select ...

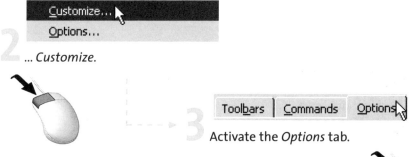

2 … *Customize.*

Activate the *Options* tab.

This is where you can customize the appearance of your screen. The toolbars are either tiled vertically or horizontally.

Vertically or horizontally?

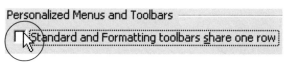

Effect on screen:

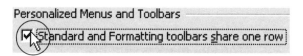

Effect on screen:

21

If there is a tick mark in front of the entry, click it. This causes the toolbars to be tiled horizontally.

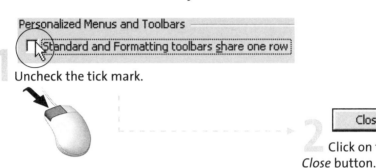

Personalized Menus and Toolbars

Standard and Formatting toolbars share one row

1 Uncheck the tick mark.

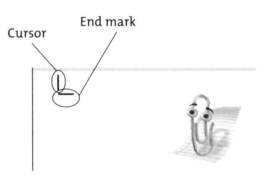

Close

2 Click on the *Close* button.

You will also see the work area on screen. The white area is where you will enter **text**. The blinking vertical bar (the **cursor**) marks the point at which the text will appear.

Cursor

End mark

The **cursor** indicates the current on-screen position by means of a flashing vertical bar. It marks the point where entered text will appear next. In Word it is called the **insertion point**.

The **end mark** is significant: It indicates that at this point your letter (also called a **document**) is finished. In a typewriter the end mark would be the bottom of an inserted sheet of paper.

Pay attention to appearances!

The mouse pointer indicates where you are currently pointing with the mouse. It communicates with you (in sign language) and informs you about what you are able to do at that moment – execute commands, or make entries via the keyboard.

Its appearance changes according to its position on the screen. If your mouse pointer is in the **command area** it will appear as an arrow. Now you can execute actions such as SAVE and PRINT.

Conversely, if you position the mouse pointer on the **work sheet**, it will change its appearance into an insertion point. Now you can enter text and/or numbers.

Move the mouse pointer across the command area ...

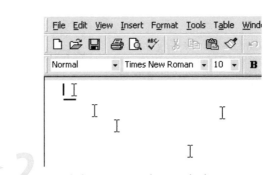

... and then across the work sheet.

Activating and deactivating toolbars

There are various toolbars in the command area.

TIP

While reading this book, you will find out a lot more about the individual toolbars when you work with the corresponding commands!

One question often posed by beginners is: "Do I really have to know the names of all these toolbars?" The only answer to this question is: Yes!

Just consider this example taken from practice.

When you are taking driving lessons, you have to know what is meant by 'clutch, brakes and accelerator' when your driving instructor uses these terms. Nobody ever says: "Now slowly release the first pedal from the left!"

Some toolbars may or may not be present on screen (especially if several people share one computer).

In Word 2000 you can **activate** or **deactivate** individual toolbars by means of the TOOLBARS option in the VIEW menu.

TIP

Standard and **formatting** should be checked. This means that they are activated. Clicking on an entry switches off the respective toolbar on your screen.

CAUTION

Standard and **formatting toolbars** should be activated on your screen. They significantly speed up some Word commands.

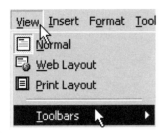

1 Open the VIEW menu, and then point the mouse at TOOLBARS.

2 Click on STANDARD in the submenu you just opened.

3 Repeat every single step of the process with the FORMATTING entry.

The two toolbars have disappeared from your screen. Incidentally, repeating the same series of actions reactivates them.

An alternative option: place the mouse pointer anywhere on any toolbar and press the right mouse button.

A menu appears – a **context menu**, to be precise – in which you can also activate or deactivate the toolbars.

25

The name **context menu** refers to the fact that the composition of the individual menu items depends on what you are doing when you press the right mouse button. Each command can also be executed via the menu bar.

In this example, move the mouse pointer over the menu bar.

Press the right mouse button: a **context menu** opens.

Click on the STANDARD entry.

Repeat every single step for the FORMATTING entry.

The toolbars – in this case standard and formatting – are again visible on your screen.

ScreenTips for beginners

Word helps you get better acquainted with the individual commands of the standard and formatting toolbars.

Leave the mouse pointer positioned on any of the buttons.

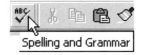

After a second **ScreenTips** are displayed.

You receive a brief message (an **on-screen tip**) about what would happen if you were to click on the button with the mouse.

If ScreenTips are not displayed, you should activate them with the following actions. This will help you get used to Word and memorise the toolbar functions more quickly.

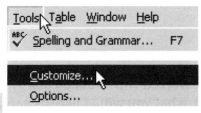

Click on Tools, then on the *Customize...* entry.

27

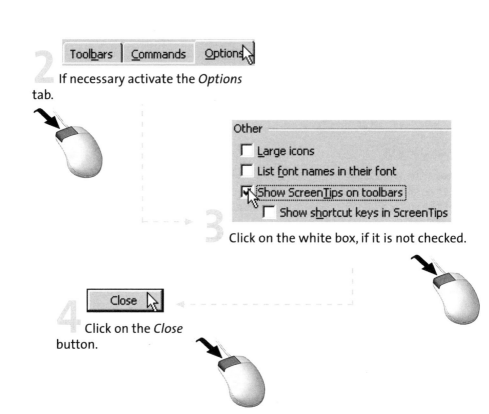

If necessary activate the *Options* tab.

Click on the white box, if it is not checked.

Click on the *Close* button.

Place the mouse pointer – without pressing the mouse buttons – on a button. The result: ScreenTips are displayed.

A tick appears next to the field after it has been clicked with the left mouse button: the function has been activated.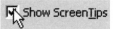

What is a dialog box?

With the help of **dialog boxes** individual Word commands are specified in more detail, and general program settings are defined or changed.

You have just worked with a **dialog box**. Here you tell Word what you would like to change (in this case, displaying of ScreenTips).

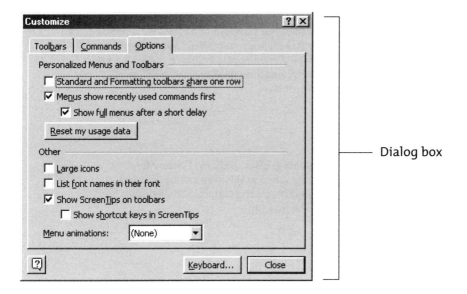

Dialog box

What are tabs?

During the last procedure you have, for the first time within this book, worked with tabs. These are operated in the same way as a **card index.**

To lay out **dialog boxes** more clearly, many of them are designed as a kind of card index box containing various cards with their tabs showing on top.

Instead of leafing through the cards, you simply click on the **tab** of the required card with the mouse. The card is then automatically moved to the front.

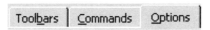

Formatting marks

After you have left the dialog box, Word reappears on your screen. With a click on the appropriate button, the **formatting marks** can be displayed.

¶

1 Click on the ¶ *Show/ Hide* button.

My·first·line·of·text¶

2 Enter text.

About dots and full stops

In the text you can see dots between the words you entered. These are not the same as full stops. They will **not be printed** and are only visible on the screen.

These symbols allow you to see more clearly the exact structure of the text and what has been done to it.

My first line of text
⌄
?

1 Without this function it is difficult to detect whether you have accidentally entered a double space .

My·first·line·⌀f··text

Two spaces

2 However, when the ¶ *Show/Hide* button is activated, you immediately notice the error.

You get to the next line by pressing the ⏎ key.

My·first·line·of·text¶
¶

1 Press the ⏎ key.

My·first·line·of·text¶
My·second·line·of·text¶

2 Type in some more text.

3 ¶
On the screen you will notice this strange character.

On the following pages of the book, these characters show you exactly when the ⏎ or the ▭ keys are pressed.

Experience shows that beginners find it difficult to get used to these characters. However, leave them activated. In this way you always see which keys have been pressed in a text.

31

The Zoom function

You can **enlarge** and **reduce** the view on your **screen** by means of the **zoom**. Please note: the font size is not changed in your print-out. The function is only used to achieve a better **on-screen** display. Think of it as the zoom on a camera or on binoculars. You can use it to bring subjects closer to you. In reality, however, the subject does not change its actual size.

If you do not see the zoom field on your screen, please refer to the steps outlined in the "Formatting marks" section.

Use the TOOLS/CUSTOMIZE menu option to display the standard and formatting toolbars one above the other by clicking on the checkmark in front of *Standard and formatting toolbar share one line*, or integrate the zoom field via the *More buttons* button.

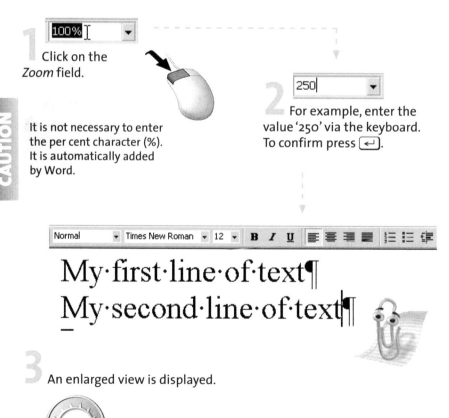

1 Click on the *Zoom* field.

It is not necessary to enter the per cent character (%). It is automatically added by Word.

2 For example, enter the value '250' via the keyboard. To confirm press ⏎.

My·first·line·of·text¶
My·second·line·of·text¶

3 An enlarged view is displayed.

A **dropdown list** only becomes visible when you click on the button with the downwards pointing arrow. Then you can select one element from the provided list.

A further option to adjust the zoom: click on the arrow next to the number. A *dropdown-list* opens. Simply select the required zoom value from the list of choices.

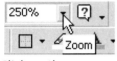

1 Click on the arrow.

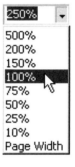

2 Select '100 %'.

33

Take a break or go on to the next chapter?

Do you wish to stop working on your computer and **exit** Word via the menu option FILE/EXIT? As you have not yet entered anything of importance, you don't need to save.

Saving means that you can go on working with this text/document when you next start up Word. (You will learn more about this in Chapter 5, 'Saving and printing')

Do you want to continue with the next chapter? Then click on the FILE/CLOSE menu option. In practice, this is comparable to removing a sheet of paper from a typewriter.

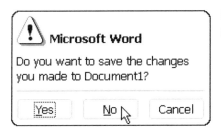

For the reasons outlined above, you do not need to save at this point.

Click on the *New* button. This is the same as inserting a second new sheet of paper into a typewriter.

What's in this chapter:

If you never make any mistakes, you can skip this chapter. However, making mistakes is only human. This chapter tells you how to correct mistakes quickly and efficiently. Once you have read it, you will be able to handle Word's spelling checker with ease.

Macking Nistakes Iss Humen

You already know about:

Starting Word   10
Choosing an Assistant   12
Exiting Word   15
The structure of Word   20
The Zoom function   32

You are going to learn about:

Correcting mistakes via
    the keyboard   38
The Word spelling checker   40

Correcting mistakes via the keyboard

For an example, you intend to write the word 'mistake'. You type 'mit' and notice that you have made a mistake. The ⌫ key deletes the **characters typed in last**, one at a time, moving left from the position of the insertion point.

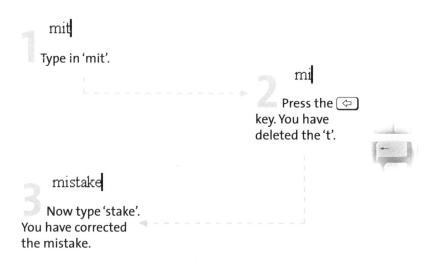

1 mit|

Type in 'mit'.

2 mi|

Press the ⌫ key. You have deleted the 't'.

3 mistake|

Now type 'stake'. You have corrected the mistake.

If you have written whole text passages, it does not make sense to press ⌫. Or perhaps you need to insert **missing letters** into words.

1 mistake¶
mitake¶

Press the ↵ key. Type in the word 'mitake', deliberately misspelling it.

2 mitake

Click in front of the 't'.

3 mis|ake

Type the missing
letter 's'. You have
corrected the mistake.

You can also correct a mistake simply by replacing one letter
with another.

1 mittake|

Press the
[↵] key.
Type the word
'mittake'.

2 m|ttake

Click in front
of the first 't'.

Here the first 't' is superfluous and should to be **overwritten** with an
's'. To do so you need the **overwrite mode**. This is toggled on and off
by pressing the
[Ins] key.

At 2.5cm   Ln 1   Col 1   REC TRK EXT OVR

Whether the
overwrite mode
is activated or

OVR = overwrite mode

not is displayed on the bottom of your screen. To switch it on:

1 Press the [Ins]
key.

2 OVR

The overwrite mode
is switched on.

39

When '**OVR**' is shown simply enter the correct letter 's'.

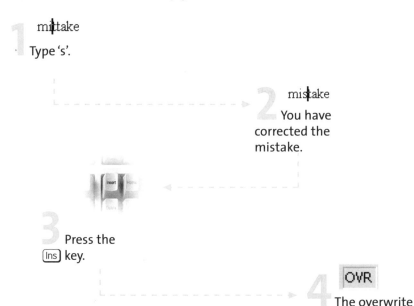

1 mi|take

Type 's'.

2 mis|ake

You have corrected the mistake.

3 Press the [Ins] key.

4 OVR

The overwrite mode is switched off.

The Word spelling checker

Word automatically underlines all misspelled words with a red wavy line, as soon as you press the ⊂⊃ or the ⏎ key after typing a word.

1 mistake¶

Press the ⏎ key.

2 Nistake¶

Type in 'mistake' deliberately misspelling it as 'Nistake'.

3 Nistake

Press the 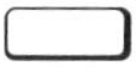 bar.

The wavy red line which appears will not be printed. It only indicates that this word is **wrong** according to Word.

1 Macking Nistakes

Type in the sentence ...

2 Macking Nistakes Iss Humen

... deliberately wrongly.

Word gives you the option to check your spelling while entering text or after you have entered it.

1 Nistakes

Click on the word 'Nistakes'.

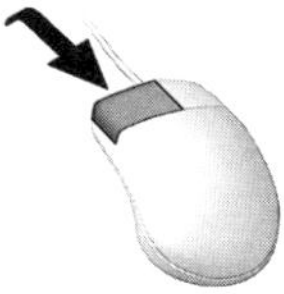

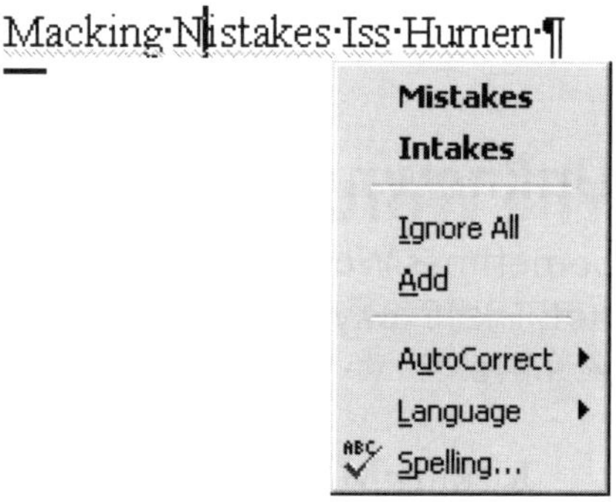
Macking Nistakes Iss Humen ¶
Mistakes
Intakes
Ignore All
Add
AutoCorrect
Language
Spelling...

2 Press the right mouse button.

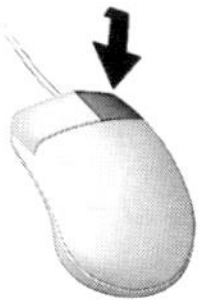

Word suggests spellings, which you may choose to adopt.

Click on 'mistake'.

Ma|cking·Mistakes·Iss·Humen·¶

Perform these steps ...

Making·Mistakes·Is·Human·

... for all remaining misspelled words.

Unknown words

Sometimes Word considers words to be misspelled when they are not. These may be proper nouns like your name or the place where you live.

Making·Mistakes·Is·Human·¶
¶

Press the ⏎ key.

I·live·in·48·Delph·Lane.

Enter the above sentence.

Here, 'Delph Lane' has been spelled correctly. However, the software rejects the expression because it is a **proper name** and thus **unknown**. Word suggests some spellings. As the street name is spelled correctly, you do not wish to accept these.

You have a choice between *Ignore All* or *Add*. With the first command you instruct Word that the expression 'Delph Lane' is correct and is not to be marked as misspelled in this document.

By selecting *Add* you choose that this name should always be accepted as correct. This means that it will be accepted as correct not only in this letter, but also in any letters you may write in the future.

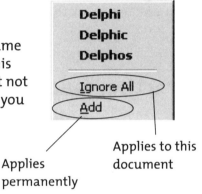

Delphi
Delphic
Delphos

Ignore All
Add

Applies permanently

Applies to this document

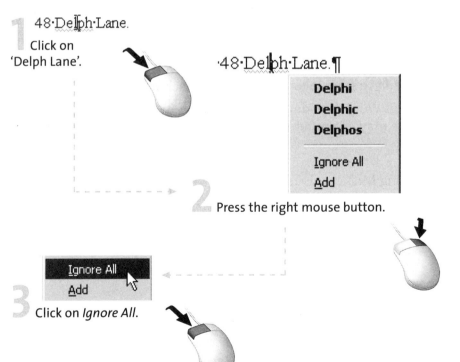

1 48·Delph·Lane.
Click on 'Delph Lane'.

·48·Delph·Lane.¶

Delphi
Delphic
Delphos

Ignore All
Add

2 Press the right mouse button.

Ignore All
Add

3 Click on *Ignore All*.

43

Hiding the wavy lines

If the automatically inserted red wavy lines irritate you, you can hide them on the *Spelling & Grammar* tab in the Tools/Options menu option.

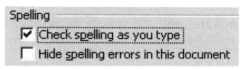

You can also check the spelling with the 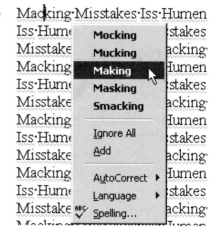 button later on.

Practise, practise ... and practise again!

Practice makes you Word-perfect!

Exercise I

Decide whether these statements are (t)rue or (f)alse. You can check the answers in the Appendix.

( ) If you adopt the word 'mistake', you correct all misspelled words.

( ) With *Add* this mistake will be

If you need to check German text (for example, when you are writing to your German (business) partner or prepare an international brochure), you can specify in the *Spelling & Grammar* tab whether

☑ Use German post-reform rules

German post-reform rules should be applied or not.

Exercise II

Word·IN·NO·TIME·facillitates·your·netry·into·tex·processing·with·Word·2000.·On· teh·basis·of·numeros·exampels·you·get·acquainted·with·the·individuel·functions.¶

Type the text **deliberately wrong**. If you wish you can insert individual mistakes of your own. Correct the misspelled words.

Word IN NO TIME facilitates your entry into text processing with Word 2000. On the basis of numerous examples you get acquainted with the individual functions.

You will notice that Word cannot cope with very badly misspelled expressions.

Take a break or go on to the next chapter?

Do you wish to stop working on your computer and **exit** Word via the menu option FILE/EXIT? As you have not yet entered anything of importance, you don't need to save.

Do you want to continue with the next chapter? Then click on the FILE/CLOSE menu option.

You do not need to save at this point.

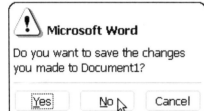

N New Blank Document

Click on the *New* button to open a new blank document.

What's in this chapter:

You are writing your first text. To prevent
readers from overlooking important points
like a meeting place or an appoint-ment
you can highlight these: **bold**, *italic*,
underlined, and so on. However, how do you
remove such formatting again? This
chapter will deal with formatting text. It
also discusses the different
fonts in Word.
You will be
surprised at
how many
formatting
options are
available to you.

abulish, attempts are currently made for paper to be re
find the good old habit of b   ng **Paper** merely post
ighest **REGARD**   office does however i
electronic Wor   document processing
irk of the Enterpri   mander of a Starship
ently smiling **Lieutenant Uhura** *simply a video ve*
ast ISDN and modern **Pentium PC**'s price-performanc

You already know about:

Starting Word   10
Choosing an Assistant   12
Exiting Word   15
The Zoom function   32
The Word spelling checker   40

You are going to learn about:

Formatting text   50
Other formatting options   53
Formatting via the keyboard   55
Fonts: types and sizes   56
Removing formatting   58
Aligning text   59
Line spacing   60

Formatting text

Text and numbers can be formatted by highlighting characters using bold or italic font styles or by under-lining them.

Characters can be highlighted by making them bold, by underlining them, and so on. In Word these procedures are called **formatting**. The necessary tools can be found in the formatting toolbar.

You can apply formatting **before or after entering text**.

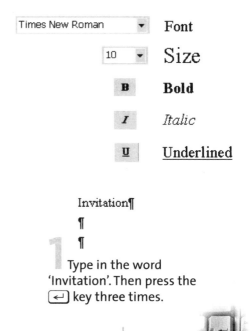

Type in the word 'Invitation'. Then press the ↵ key three times.

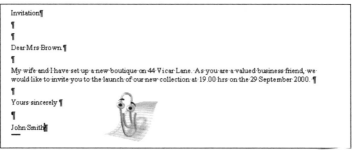

Type the whole letter:

'Dear Mrs Brown

My wife and I have set up a new boutique at 44 Vicar Lane. As you are a valued customer, we would like to invite you to the launch of our new collection at 19.00 hrs on 29 September 2000.

Yours sincerely

John Smith'

Highlighting individual words

If you want to format a **single** word, it's easiest to just **click on** it.

In Word a single word consists of the characters between two spaces.

In this example you will use italic: *a script which tilts slightly to the right*.

1 Click on the word 'launch'.

2 Format the word by clicking on the button *Italic* now on the formatting toolbar.

Marking/selecting text

You select text whenever you want to highlight **more than one word**. There are several options, the quickest of which is to use the **mouse**. Place the mouse pointer in front of the word. Holding down the left mouse button drag it across the words you want to mark.

1 Click in front of '44'.

2

44·Vicar·Lane.

Holding down the left mouse button, drag the mouse to the right.

3 44·Vicar·Lane

Now try the street name 'Vicar Lane'.

4

Bold

Click on the *Bold* button.

5 ique·on·**44·Vicar·Lane**.·As·yo
·of our·new·collection·at·19.00

By clicking anywhere on the document you can remove the selection again.

If you still find working with the mouse difficult, use the keyboard.
Position the cursor in front of the words you wish to select.
Press the ⬆ key and hold it down. Operate the → key until you have
selected the appropriate words.
More options for selecting text are outlined in the Appendix
'Quick text selection with the mouse'.

Other formatting options

Apart from bold, italic, and underline there are other formatting options in the FORMAT/FONT menu. Via the *Font* tab, you can also double underline words or use superscript or subscript.

Instead of the FORMAT/FONT menu command you can press the Ctrl+D keys, thus directly accessing the dialog box.

The action of simultaneously pressing two or more keys is called a **keyboard shortcut**. A keyboard shortcut executes one particular function.

Example:

You wish to double underline the date '29 September 2000'.

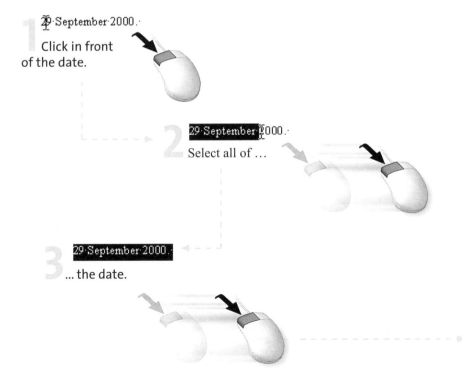

1 29·September·2000.·

Click in front of the date.

2 29·September·2000.·

Select all of …

3 29·September·2000.·

… the date.

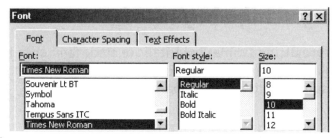

4 Press the keyboard shortcut Ctrl+D which will activate the *Font* tab.

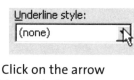

5 Click on the arrow next to *Underline*.

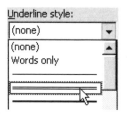

6 Select the *Double* item.

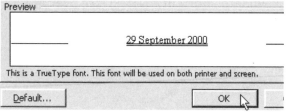

7 Now look at the preview and confirm your choice with the *OK* button.

Formatting via the keyboard

You can apply formatting such as bold, italic or, underlining via the formatting toolbar or by selecting the FORMAT/FONT menu option. To achieve the same effects with **keyboard shortcuts**, see below.

Keyboard shortcuts for formatting

Formatting	Keyboard shortcut
Bold	Ctrl + ⇧ + F
Italic	Ctrl + ⇧ + K
Superscript	Ctrl + +
Subscript	Ctrl + #
Small caps	Ctrl + ⇧ + Q
All caps	Ctrl + ⇧ + G
Underline	Ctrl + ⇧ + U
Double underline	Ctrl + ⇧ + D
Remove all formatting	Ctrl + ⬚

Apply superscript

The time 19.00 hrs has to be formatted in such a way that the final two zeros are underlined and raised at the same time. You can format the characters via the FORMAT/FONT menu option on the *Font* tab or press the keyboard shortcut Ctrl + + (see overview).

1 19.00 hrs·

Click between the full stop (.) and the second zero.

2 Mark 'oo'.

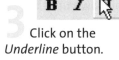

3 Click on the *Underline* button.

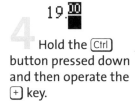

4 Hold the `Ctrl` button pressed down and then operate the `+` key.

Fonts: types and sizes

In Word you have the option to change font as well as type size. There are numerous ways of doing this.

1 Click on the word 'Invitation'.

2 On the formatting toolbar open the drop-down list of fonts by clicking on the arrow.

3 Scroll down until the 'Arial' font appears.

Activate the 'Arial' font.

4

Fonts are **sorted alphabetically**.

5 On the formatting bar open the drop-down list of type sizes by clicking on the arrow.

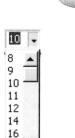

Select '20'.

6

Try out different options in this way.

57

Removing formatting

Formatting is removed by clicking on the term.

Invitation¶

1 If necessary click on the word 'Invitation'.

2 Keeping the [Ctrl] button pressed down, press the [   ] bar.

Invitation¶

3 Font and type size have been removed by Word.

Alternatively formatting can be removed by clicking on the respective button.

44 Vicar Lane

1 Highlight '44 Vicar Lane'.

B *I* <u>U</u>

Bold

2 Clicking on the *Bold* button removes the text formatting.

ique·on·44]Vicar·Lane.·As
of·our·new·collection·at·1S

3 Clicking your mouse anywhere
in the document drops the selection.

Aligning text

In Word you can align text in different ways. You may align text **left**,
right, or **centred**. For example, in order to highlight the reference of a
letter, you can centre it in the document.

Invitation¶

1 Click on the
word 'Invitation'.

Center

2 On the formatting
toolbar select the
Center button.

Justify

Another button on the toolbar is **Justify**.
This **justifies** text to the left-hand and right-hand
margins of the document.

Justify

The length of text lines is hardly ever identical.

Example:
Aligned left

Yesterday I went for a walk through a dark forest. Suddenly a UFO landed right in front of me. The door opened and a monster with a moustache approached me. "Please release me let me go, for I don't love you anymore ..." the strange creature said to me in a pained tone of voice. It was terrible. Never in my life I have heard anything quite as terrible.

Justify remedies this failing. This formatting is frequently used in books, newspapers and magazines.

Example:
Justified

Yesterday I went for a walk through a dark forest. Suddenly a UFO landed right in front of me. The door opened and a monster with a moustache approached me. "Please release me let me go, for I don't love you anymore ..." the strange creature said to me in a pained tone of voice. It was terrible. Never in my life I have heard anything quite as terrible.

Line spacing

Word also allows you to specify the line spacing in your document. Holding down the ⌈Ctrl⌉ key, press the appropriate number on your keyboard.

Key	Function
⌈Ctrl⌉+⌈1⌉	**Single** line space
⌈Ctrl⌉+⌈2⌉	**Double** line space
⌈Ctrl⌉+⌈5⌉	**1.5** line spacing

My wife and I have set up a new boutique on 44 Vicar Lane. A would like to invite you to the launch of our new collection at 1

 Click anywhere within the text of the letter.

My wife and I have set up a new boutique on 44 Vicar Lane

would like to invite you to the launch of our new collection

2 Holding the `Ctrl` key down, press the `2` key.

My wife and I have set up a new boutique on 44 Vicar Lane. A
would like to invite you to the launch of our new collection at 1

3 Return to single line spacing via the keyboard shortcut `Ctrl`+`1`.

This time do not exit Word! In the next
chapter you will learn about **saving and
printing**. Use this text for the exercise.

5

What's in this chapter:

If you intend to continue with your work tomorrow, the day after tomorrow, next year, in the next millennium, would you leave on the PC all the time in order to save your text? If so, your power supplier would be ecstatic! You don't have to of course – in this chapter you learn about saving letters, both on your computer's hard drive and on diskette. You print out the text as necessary. However, before you do so you may wish to check the print-out by using Print Preview, in case you need to amend your document, thus saving paper.

Dear Ms Brown

My wife and I have set up a new boutique at 44 invite you to the launch of our new collection at

Yours sincerely

You already know about:

Starting Word   10
Choosing an Assistant   12
The Zoom function   32
The Word spelling checker   40
Formatting text   50
Other formatting options   53

You are going to learn about:

Saving text   64
Saving changes   69
Save or Save As...?   70
Saving to diskette   72
Print Preview   75
Printing a document   76
The 'Full Screen' view   78

Saving text

You need to be able to save your work on your computer, so that you can continue working on it at a later date.

The title bar

The title bar tells you which document you are currently editing.

In Word the pages you work with are called a **document**.

Treat a document as a paper one which may consist of one or more pages.

Every document is given a name. In Word this is done using the **Save** function.

Not yet saved — First document you have opened in your current session

If the word **Document** is displayed on the title bar, this means that you have not yet saved your work. This name is automatically assigned by Word.

The number **1** behind the term 'document' tells you that you are currently working on the first document you opened in your current working sessions.

An example from everyday office practice:

Practice	Terms used in Word
Paper/document	Document
Documents **without a name**	**Not saved**, the term 'Document' is assigned
Documents **with names** (as with files)	**Saved**, a name is assigned

Saving a document on your computer

Do you still have the 'Invitation' from Chapter 4?

Invitation

Dear Mrs Brown

My wife and I have set up a new boutique on 44 Vicar Lane. As you are a valued business friend, we
would like to invite you to the launch of our new collection at 19.00 hrs on the 29 September 2000.

Yours sincerely

John Smith

If not, simply type in any kind of text. It does not matter as this section is about understanding the *Save* and the *Print* function.

You **save** a document, in order to file it permanently on the hard disk of your computer.

Generally the **hard disk** is a built-in storage device which permits you to store large amounts of data even if the computer is not switched on.

WHAT'S THIS?

An example to make it clearer:

Everyday office practice	Word
Assigning a name to a document	Assigning a file name
Putting the document into a ring-binder	Saving and filing the document
Closing the ring-binder	Exiting Word

To **Save** a document you can either click on the button with the diskette symbol or call up the FILE/SAVE menu option.

Click on the *Save* button.

Save As

Save in: [ ] My Documents   ▼

The *Save As* dialog box opens.

In *File name* you specify the **name** under which you want to store the document.

Everything you create and save with a Windows program such as Word or Excel becomes a file.

Word automatically suggests the name 'Invitation.doc', since 'Invitation is the first word the document contains, and where '**.doc**' (an abbrevia-tion for document) represents the **Word** software. This file 'extension' is assigned by the program and need not be entered at later stages.

The name 'Invitation.doc' should – if you have not done anything else – still be high-lighted by Word. You can simply overwrite it.

File name: Invitation.doc

Save as type: Word Document (*.doc)

Example:

The letter is addressed to a Ms Brown. Choose 'Brown' as the file name.

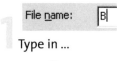

File name: B|

Type in ...

File name: | Brown|

... the file name
' Brown'.

File name: | Invitation.doc

If the term 'Invitation.doc' is **not highlighted**,
double-click on the term 'Invitation' with the
left mouse button. Then it will be highlighted
and you can overwrite it.

In *Save in* you specify **where** you
want to store the document.
Word automatically suggests
the folder 'My Documents'.
However, it is also possible to
specify a different **location**, and
I will discuss this later.

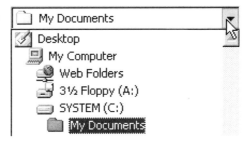

- My Documents
- Desktop
  - My Computer
  - Web Folders
  - 3½ Floppy (A:)
  - SYSTEM (C:)
    - My Documents

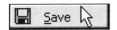

Click on the *Save* button.

Dear Mrs Brown

My wife and I have set up a new boutique on
would like to invite you to the launch of our r

Yours sincerely

John Smith

This takes you back to the document.

67

Look at the very top of your screen! On the title bar you now see the name 'Brown.doc'.

All of this information is now stored inside the document.

File name

Extension **.doc** (abbreviation for **doc**ument). The file is a document.

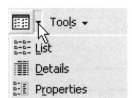

In the *Save As* dialog box you are provided with additional information.

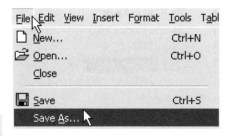

Call up the FILE/SAVE AS ... menu command.

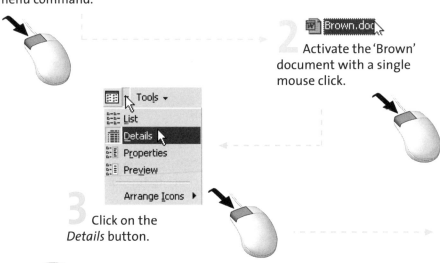

Activate the 'Brown' document with a single mouse click.

Click on the *Details* button.

Or click on the *Properties* button.

Leave the dialog box with the *Cancel* Button.

Saving changes

TIP

When you exit Word, the program asks whether you wish to save the changes you have made.

What happens when you alter the data in the document?

If you intend to go on working with word, a mouse click on the *Save* button is enough.

ɪ a new boutiqu
ɔ the launch of (

Click in front of the word 'boutique'.

new fashion boutique on

Type the word 'fashion'.

69

Save the changes.

The entire modified text is saved by Word.

Save or Save As ... ?

.. that is the question. What is the difference between *Save* and the FILE/SAVE AS menu command?

If you modify a document and subsequently save it the original data has disappeared and/or new data has been added.

Click in front of the family name 'Brown'.

Dear Mrs Ethel Brown

Type in the first name 'Ethel'.

Click on the *Save* button.

The change is now permanently stored in the document 'Brown'. What is the purpose of the FILE/SAVE AS menu option then?

Dear Mrs Ethel⌐Brown

Click in front of the name 'Ethel Brown'.

Dear Mrs Paula Miller

Change it to 'Paula Miller'.

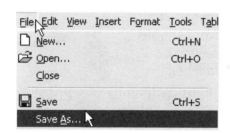

Select the FILE/SAVE AS menu option.

File name: Miller|

Enter 'Miller' as the file name.

Activate the *Save* button.

📝 Miller.doc - Microsoft Word

The letter to Mrs Miller has been saved by Word as you can see on the title bar!

Instead of selecting the FILE/SAVE AS menu option you can press the F12 key. This is an alternative way to open the *Save As* dialog box.

The above document is now saved on the hard disk of your computer.

71

Saving to diskette

Occasionally you may wish to save your document on a diskette for security reasons or because you want to use the file on a different computer.

Via a floppy disk drive **diskettes** can record and permanently store data. The data can then be read by different computers.

The common size of diskettes is 3.5 inches. The front should always be labelled.

It is possible to write-protect diskettes. Whenever the little black tab on the back is up (that is, it is possible to look through the 'little window' thus created), it is only possible to read from the diskette and not to write to it.

In this example you want to save the text on diskette, so you leave the tab in the down position.

On the front of the diskette you will notice an arrow. Following its direction you insert the diskette into the floppy disk drive of your computer.

Never force a diskette into a disk drive!

Insert the diskette into the floppy disk drive of your computer until it clicks into place.

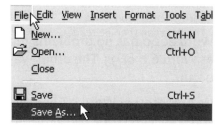

Select the FILE/SAVE AS menu option.

File name: [Invitation on diskette]

Type in 'Invitation on diskette' as the file name.

On most computers the floppy disk drive is referred to as 'A:'.

Save in: [My Documents]

Under *Save As...*

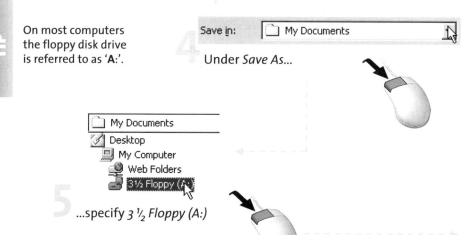

...specify *3 ½ Floppy (A:)*

73

6 Click on the *Save* button. The document is now on your diskette.

Word 2000 has no problems reading files of older versions such as Word 6.0 or 95. The other way round, however, problems may occur.

Its predecessor Word 97, however, can read Word 2000 files. Only some special Word 2000 formatting will be lost.

CAUTION

If you wish to save text on a diskette for somebody who only has an **older version** of Word on his or her computer, you can specify this under *Save as type* in the *Save As* dialog box.

TIP

How to reopen the document on the diskette will be outlined in Chapter 6 on 'Accessing, saving and deleting documents'!

Print Preview

Before you print out a document you should check it using Print Preview as you might want to modify its appearance.

You find **Print Preview** in the FILE menu. You can access it even more quickly with the relevant button on the standard toolbar.

One click and you are in **Print Preview**, which displays what the printed document will look like.

With the magnifying glass you can magnify or reduce the view of a document. The appearance of a future print-out is not affected by this.

You return to the original document by pressing the [Esc] key or clicking on the *Close* button.

CAUTION

It is not possible to enter data in **Print Preview** mode.

Click on the *Print Preview* button.

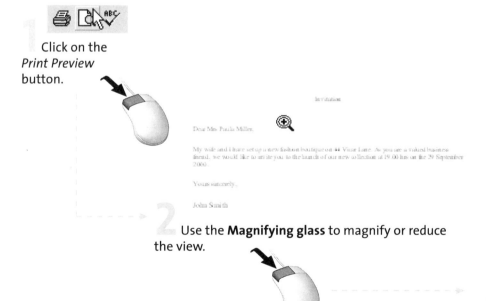

Use the **Magnifying glass** to magnify or reduce the view.

Invitation

Dear Mrs Paula Miller

My wife and I have set up a new fashion boutique on 44 V
friend, we would like to invite you to the launch of our ne
2000.

Yours sincerely

3 You see a preview of the subsequent print-out.

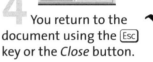

4 You return to the
document using the [Esc]
key or the *Close* button.

Printing a document

When you select the *Print* button, the document will be printed out
on paper.

1 Select the
Print button.

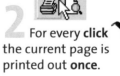

If a document is printed
without specifying a
page range, Word prints
all non-empty pages.

2 For every **click**
the current page is
printed out **once**.

In addition, the FILE/PRINT menu command is available for printing
documents.

Only the selection is printed   Printer selection   Number of copies to be printed

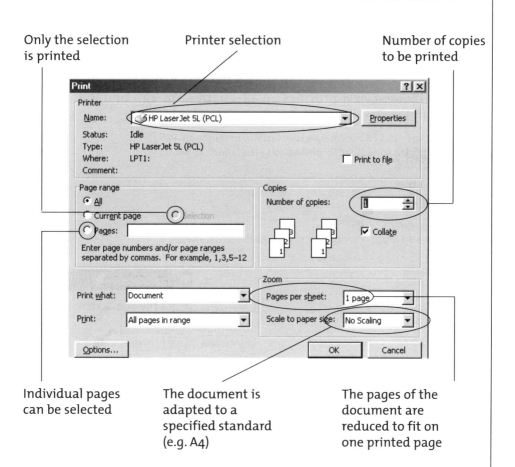

Individual pages can be selected   The document is adapted to a specified standard (e.g. A4)   The pages of the document are reduced to fit on one printed page

In the *Print* dialog box you can specify further details. Here you can determine how many copies of the document you want, or which printer you want to carry out the job, if you have a choice of printers.

The 'Full Screen' view

Occasionally the screen detail shown in Word is not big enough. The **Full Screen** view provides an alternative. You can find this command in the VIEW menu.

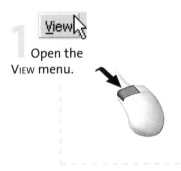

1 Open the VIEW menu.

2 Select the FULL SCREEN command.

The screen detail of the document has been enlarged. For now the toolbars have disappeared from the screen.

In FULL SCREEN view the **menu bar** appears when you move the mouse pointer to the top of the screen.

1 Press the [Esc] key.

2 You return to Word's normal view.

Exit Word! Your documents have been saved. The next chapter teaches you how to access saved documents.

CAUTION

If you intend to switch off your PC, **do not** forget to remove the diskette you have used in this chapter from the floppy disk drive.

79

6

What's in this chapter:

Do you now wish to continue with yesterday's, last week's, or last year's work? In the previous chapter you learnt how to store (save) documents. But how do you get saved documents back onto your screen?

This chapter shows you how to access (open) existing documents; how to protect your documents to prevent unauthorised access to your personal   data, and how to delete the   files you don't
                                                 need anymore.

Dear Mrs Brown

My wife and I have set up a new boutique on 44 Vicar Lane. As you are a valued
would like to invite you to the launch of our new collection at 19.00 hrs on the 2

Yours sincerely

You already know about:

Starting Word   10
The Zoom function   32
The Word spelling checker   40
Formatting text   50
Saving text   64
Saving changes   69
Saving to diskette   72
Print Preview   75
Printing a document   76

You are going to learn about:

Accessing documents   82
Protecting data from
        unauthorised access   87
Deleting documents   92

Accessing documents

The **process of accessing** a document is referred to as **opening it**.

In order to open a document in Word, it needs first to be saved (as outlined in Chapter 5).

Afterwards you may not need to use this document for days or even weeks.

This chapter shows you how to continue working with a saved document.

An illustration to make it clearer:

Everyday office practice	Word
Opening a ring-binder	Starting Word
Extracting a document	Opening a document

You have already opened the ring-binder and now all that remains to do is extract the document.

Click on the *Open* button or select the FILE/OPEN menu option in Word. Both methods take you to the same dialog box.

Example

You want to open the document 'Invitation on diskette', which you have saved on diskette in the last chapter.

In *Look in* you specify **where** the document is located. In the case of a **diskette** you click on '3½ Floppy (A:)'.

Insert the diskette you used in
the last chapter into the floppy disk
drive of your computer.

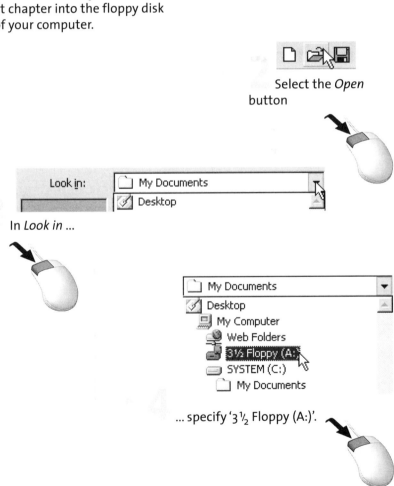

Select the *Open*
button

In *Look in* ...

... specify '3 ½ Floppy (A:)'.

83

Finally, specify the name of the document you want to open. Here it is: 'Invitation on diskette.doc'

Double-click on the **name of the file** with the left mouse button. Alternatively select it with a single click, and confirm with the *Open* button. Both methods take you back to the screen: the selected document appears.

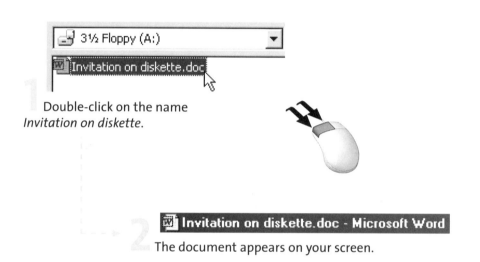

Double-click on the name
Invitation on diskette.

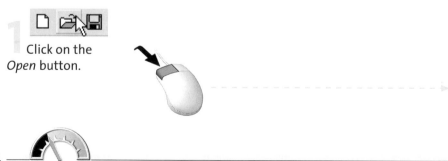

The document appears on your screen.

Of course you can also open documents which are saved on the **hard disk** of your computer.

Example

You want to open the document 'Miller', which you saved on the hard disk of your computer in the last chapter.

Click on the
Open button.

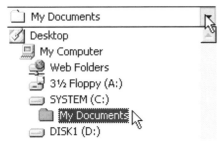

Under *Look in*, first select drive 'C', and then *My Documents*.

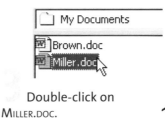

Double-click on
MILLER.DOC.

The recently used file list: the last four

At the moment the easiest way for you to open a document is probably via the FILE menu.

At the bottom of the menu you will notice the names:

'1 Miller.doc'

'2 Invitation on diskette.doc ...'

'3 Brown.doc'

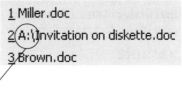

A:\ = name of the disk drive

Under the FILE menu, the four **most recently used documents** (so far you have only used three!) are listed.

When you select the menu entry BROWN, the document will open. This option is a shortcut.

85

File Edit View

Via the FILE menu ...

1 Miller.doc
2 A:\Invitation on diskette.doc
3 Brown.doc

... select the document
Brown.doc.

If you now reopen the FILE menu, you will notice that the **order** of the files has changed.

The entry 'Brown' is now at the top of the list, because it is the most recently used document.

1 Brown.doc
2 Miller.doc
3 A:\Invitation on diskette.doc

The recently used file list: the last nine

At the moment only the **last four** documents are displayed on the list.

TIP

On the *General* tab under the TOOLS/OPTIONS menu item you can increase the **number of files** on the recently used file list to a maximum of nine.

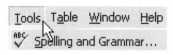

Tools Table Window Help
ABC Spelling and Grammar...

Options...

Select the TOOLS/OPTIONS menu command.

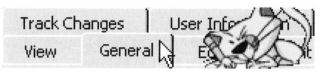

Bring the *General* tab into the foreground.

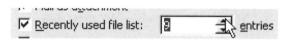

With the mouse, increase the number shown
in *Recently used files* to '9'.

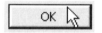

Confirm the
change with a click
on the *OK* button.

When you now open the FILE menu, nothing will have changed.
However, if you save and open a number of different documents
one after the other the nine most recently used files appear.

Protecting data from unauthorised access

The situation might arise in which you would like to keep your data
secret from other people.

You need to think up and assign a **password**.

Example

When assigning a password, please note that a difference is made between **upper** and **lower case spelling**.

At the moment the document 'Brown' is displayed on your screen. You want to protect this file from unauthorized access so that no one but you can read it. You enter the password 'EaSy'.

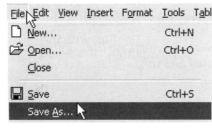

Select the FILE/SAVE As menu option.

In the dialog box, activate the *Tools* button, and then the *General Options* entry.

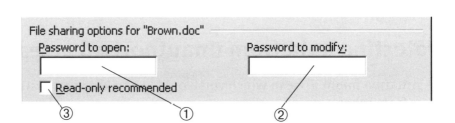

In the following dialog box you can specify whether you ...

1. ... authorise **reading and writing** (*read/write access*) or

2. allow reading only, while preventing **writing**, or modification, (*write-protection*).

3. If you mark the *Read-only recommended* control button, you will receive a corresponding **message** when you open the respective document.

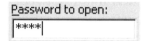

Type the password 'EaSy' into the text box.

Confirm with the
OK button.

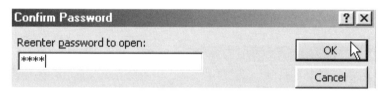

Repeat the password 'EaSy' using exactly the same spelling as before. Then confirm with the *OK* button.

Save the changes made to the document via the *Save* button.

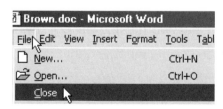

Close the document on your screen via the FILE/CLOSE menu option.

From now on it will only be possible to open the document 'Brown' using the **password** 'EaSy'.

Next time you open the document 'Brown', Word will ask you to enter the **password**. Without the password you will not be able to view the file.

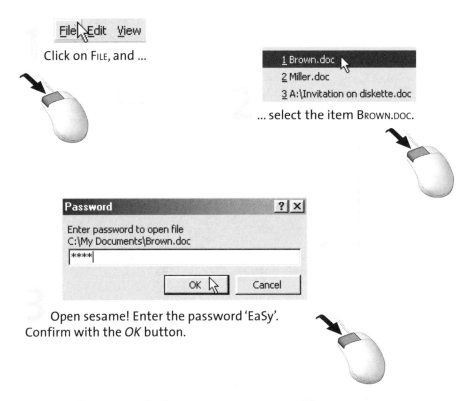

Click on FILE, and ...

1 Brown.doc
2 Miller.doc
3 A:\Invitation on diskette.doc

... select the item BROWN.DOC.

Password

Enter password to open file
C:\My Documents\Brown.doc

OK   Cancel

Open sesame! Enter the password 'EaSy'.
Confirm with the *OK* button.

How do you delete a password?

Would you like to **remove** the read and write protection from the document 'Brown'? Just delete the password using the ⌨Del key.

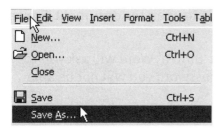

Select the FILE/SAVE AS menu option.

Activate the *Tools* button and then the *General Options* item.

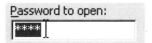

Select the keyword.

File sharing options for "Brown.doc"

Password to open:

☐ Read-only recommended

Password to modify:

OK   Cancel

Press the ⌦ key, and confirm with *OK*.

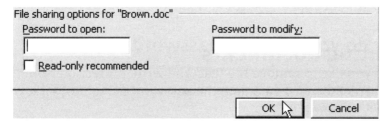

91

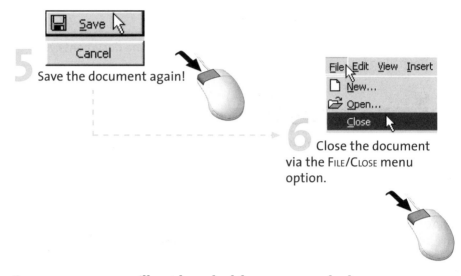

5 Save the document again!

6 Close the document via the FILE/CLOSE menu option.

From now on you will not be asked for a password when you open the document.

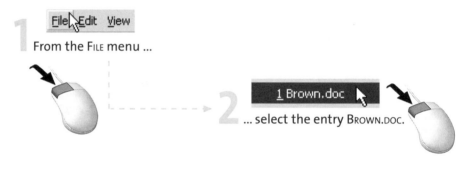

1 From the FILE menu ...

2 ... select the entry BROWN.DOC.

The document appears on your screen. Everything is back to normal.

Deleting documents

You want to delete a document because you do not need it anymore. Well, let's throw it out!

Example

The document 'Miller' is to be deleted.

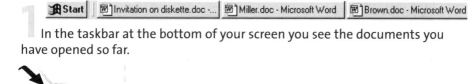

In the taskbar at the bottom of your screen you see the documents you have opened so far.

Click on the document 'Miller'. It appears on the screen.

Under the WINDOW menu you can also find the documents which are already open. Bring one of them to the foreground by clicking on the corresponding menu entry.

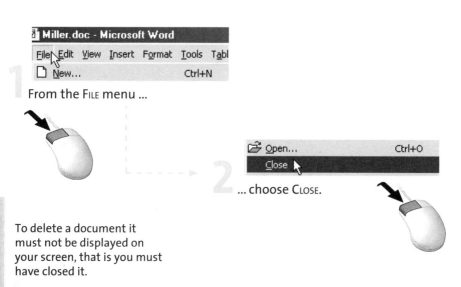

From the FILE menu ...

... choose CLOSE.

To delete a document it must not be displayed on your screen, that is you must have closed it.

The choice is yours. You can either select the *Save As* dialog box (FILE/ SAVE AS menu) or the *Open* dialog box (FILE/OPEN menu). From both dialogs you can delete an existing document/file.

93

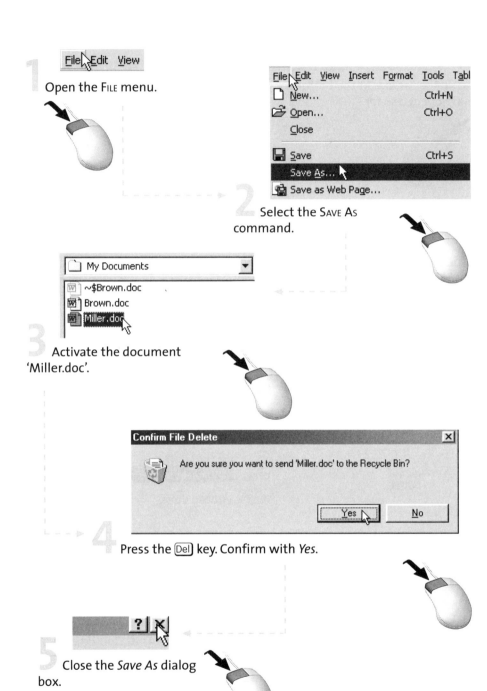

File Edit View

Open the FILE menu.

File Edit View Insert Format Tools Tabl
New...   Ctrl+N
Open...   Ctrl+O
Close

Save   Ctrl+S
Save As...
Save as Web Page...

Select the SAVE AS command.

My Documents

~$Brown.doc
Brown.doc
Miller.doc

Activate the document 'Miller.doc'.

Confirm File Delete

Are you sure you want to send 'Miller.doc' to the Recycle Bin?

Yes   No

Press the Del key. Confirm with *Yes*.

Close the *Save As* dialog box.

The document has been removed from the hard disk of your computer.

Not completely, though! There is a **recycle bin** on the desktop. It allows you to delete files permanently, but also to restore accidentally deleted files.

Practise, practise ... and practise again!

Answer the following questions. The correct answers can be found in the Appendix.

Clicking on the *Open* button and the FILE/OPEN menu option leads ...

❏ to different dialog boxes;

❏ to the *Open* dialog box;

❏ to the *Save* dialog box.

For read- and write-protection whether a password is in upper - or lower case is ...

❏ important;

❏ unimportant.

A document can only be deleted ...

❏ when it is open, i.e. currently in use;

❏ when it is not open, i.e. currently not in use.

Go through the following exercise. Carry out the intermediate steps on your own!

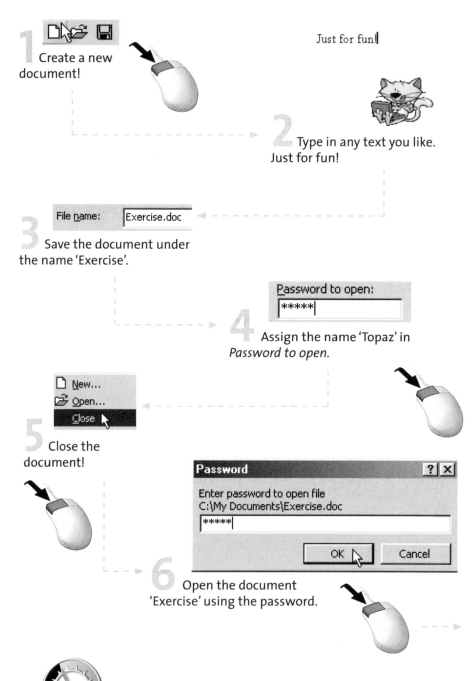

1 Create a new document!

Just for fun|

2 Type in any text you like. Just for fun!

File name: Exercise.doc

3 Save the document under the name 'Exercise'.

Password to open:
*****

4 Assign the name 'Topaz' in *Password to open*.

☐ New...
☞ Open...
Close

5 Close the document!

Password   ? ✕

Enter password to open file
C:\My Documents\Exercise.doc
*****

                    OK   Cancel

6 Open the document 'Exercise' using the password.

Password to open:
*****

7 Delete the password.

8 Close the file
'Exercise'.

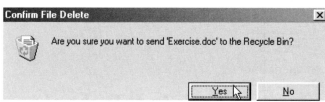

9 Delete the document.

If you are going to switch off your PC,
do not forget to remove the diskette
you have used in this chapter from the
floppy disk drive.

7

What's in this chapter:

Mr Grumpy is foaming with anger! He has
just returned from a holiday from hell
which, in his opinion, he did not deserve at
all! Everything went wrong. As soon as he
gets home, still a little irritated,
he switches on his computer. To
present his complaints clearly,
he numbers them. As soon as
he has calmed down a little he
decides to correct his letter. He
rearranges sentences and
substitutes words he has used
too frequently.

You already know about:

The Word spelling checker	40
Formatting text	50
Other formatting options	53
Saving changes	69
Saving to diskette	72
Printing a document	76
Accessing documents	82
Protecting data from unauthorised access	87
Deleting documents	92

You are going to learn about:

Creating lists	100
Moving and copying text	103
The Thesaurus	106
Finding and replacing text	111
The 'Format Painter' button	114

Creating lists

When reading a text people's attention is first drawn to lists. The most common list type is '1,2,3, ...'. There is a button in Word which allows you to create a numbered list when you click on it.

1. Dog
2. Cat
3. Mouse

- Dog
- Cat
- Mouse

Another way to create lists is to use bullets.

There are many types of lists, not limited to these two buttons. Under the FORMAT/BULLETS AND NUMBERING menu option on the *Bulleted* tab you can find many more layout styles for bullet lists, as follows.

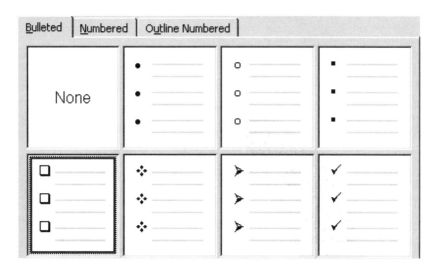

Selecting a list style

If you have already typed in your text, then highlight it, and choose a list style. However, alternatively you can select the list style first and then type in your text.

Dear Mr Greedy ¶
¶
From the 17/05 to the 27/05 I was a tenant in your house on the island of Tobaluba. Unfortunately, the house failed to meet the expected standards, as we were faced with a number of problems. It was thus impossible for us to have a nice, relaxing holiday. The following problems occurred:¶
¶
𝕀

1 Enter your text.

2 Select the *Numbering* button.

1.→ The toilets were always blocked.¶

3 Input the first line.

Word numbers it as soon as you press the ⏎ key. **The list finishes** automatically when you insert an empty line, i.e. when you hit the ⏎ key twice in succession.

2.→𝕀

4 Press the ⏎ key.

1. → The·toilets·were·always·blocked.¶
2. → The·crockery·was·missing·from·the·kitchen.¶
3. → The·cleaning·lady·came·only·once·every·three·days.¶
4. → The·sun·was·shining·for·only·five·days.¶
5. → The·water·in·the·pool·was·far·too·cold.𝕀

5 Enter the remaining items in the same way. When you have entered each item, press the ⏎ key.

5. → The·water·in·the·pool·was·far·too·cold.¶
6. → 𝕀

6 When you have entered all the items, press the ⏎ key once.

5. → The·water·in·the·pool·was·far·too·cold.¶

¶

Leave this line empty. Press the ⏎ key again.

5. → The·water·in·the·pool·was·far·too·cold.¶

¶

I·hope·to·hear·from·you·soon.¶

¶

Yours·sincerely,¶

¶

¶

John·Grumpy¶

Continue with 'normal' text inputting.

Removing a list item

It is possible to remove list items once they have been entered (as demonstrated here with 'dog, cat, mouse'). Note that the whole line has been **selected**. Move the mouse pointer in front of the list entry you want to remove. In this case it is '2. cat'. Once you have selected the line, press the Del key. The line will disappear.

1.   Dog
2.   Cat
3.   Mouse

1. Dog   The list has automatically been adapted by Word. The
2. Mouse   mouse which was number 3 is now number 2.

In our example Mr Grumpy wants to delete a list item. He concedes, after talking to his wife, that he cannot blame anybody for the bad weather. Thus, he removes item no. 4 from his list.

1. → The·toilets·were·always·blocked.¶
2. → The·crockery·was·missing·from·the·kitchen.¶
3. → The·cleaning·lady·came·only·once·every·three·days.¶
4. → The·sun·was·shining·for·only·five·days.¶
5. → The·water·in·the·pool·was·far·too·cold.¶

Position the mouse pointer in front of item 4.

1. → The·toilets·were·always·blocked.¶
2. → The·crockery·was·missing·from·the·kitchen.¶
3. → The·cleaning·lady·came·only·once·every·thre
4. → The·sun·was·shining·for·only·five·days.¶
5. → The·water·in·the·pool·was·far·too·cold.¶

Click the left mouse button to select the line.

1. → The·toilets·were·always·blocked.¶
2. → The·crockery·was·missing·from·the·kitchen.'
3. → The·cleaning·lady·came·only·once·every·thr
4. → The·water·in·the·pool·was·far·too·cold.¶

Delete the item with the ⟨Del⟩ key.

Moving and copying text

You have to **select** text first in order to **move** or **copy** it.

From·the·17/05·to·the·27/05·I·was·a·tenant·in·your·house·on·the·island·of·Tobaluba.·Unfortunately,·the·house·failed·to·meet·the·expected·standards,·as·we·were·faced·with·a·number·of·problems.·It·was·thus·impossible·for·us·to·have·a·nice,·relaxing·holiday.·The·following·problems·occurred.¶

Now click on the button with the scissors. This cuts out the selection.

If on the other hand you want to duplicate the text, you have to **copy** it.

It does not matter which button you choose, the subsequent procedure is the same. Your text is now on Word's **clipboard**.

... and pasting text

You have to place the cursor where you want to insert the text passage. Then simply click on the *Paste* button.

Moving and copying text using the mouse

Here is where the mouse comes into play! Skilled mouse operators work much more quickly. They use the **drag & drop** method.

Position the mouse pointer in front of the selection and click the left mouse button. A dotted rectangle appears below the mouse pointer. Word tells you that you can now move the selection.

1 on·the·island·of·Tobaluba

Select the text.

on·the·island·of·Tobaluba

2 Hold down the left mouse button.

In front of the mouse pointer a **dotted line** appears. Keep pressing the mouse button, while you move the dotted line to the place where you want to insert the text. Now release the mouse button.

1 Drag the text to a different place.

From the 17/05 to the 27/05 I was a tenant in your house. Unfortunately, the house failed to meet the expected standards, as we were faced with a number of problems. It was thus impossible for us to have a nice, relaxing holiday on the island of Tobaluba. The following problems occurred:

2 As soon as you release the mouse button the text is moved.

The text disappears from its old position and appears at its new one.

Incidentally, it is also possible to **copy** with the mouse. This involves exactly the same procedure as with moving text, only that additionally you have to press the ⌗Ctrl⌗ key. Here a **plus** (+) appears next to the mouse pointer.

The Thesaurus

'The house next to our house was bigger than the house across the road.' This section is about **repeatedly** using the same **words**. House, house, house. You see that this term has been used too often. Can't you think of another word? In the TOOLS/LANGUAGE submenu there is a function called **Thesaurus**. Here you can find synonyms (expressions which have a similar meaning) for words. Authors use this function quite frequently – including the author of this book.

Thus you could reword your original sentence as follows: 'The house next to our home was bigger than the building across the road.' This sounds a lot better than the first version.

From the 17/05 to the 27/05 I was a tenant in your house. Unfortunately, the house failed to meet the expected standards, as we were faced with a number of problems. It was thus impossible for us to have a nice, relaxing holiday on the island of Tobaluba. The following problems occurred:

In his letter Mr Grumpy in his overzealousness used the same words over and over again. All you need to do is position the cursor in a word and the software knows that you want to find a synonym for this word.

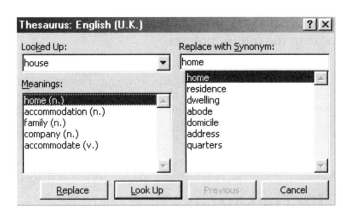

The function is accessed via the TOOLS/LANGUAGE menu option.

The house failed
Click on the word 'house'.

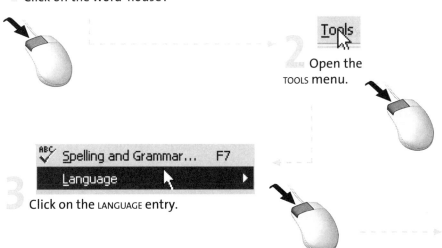

Open the TOOLS menu.

Click on the LANGUAGE entry.

4 Start the Thesaurus.

Alternatively you can start the Thesaurus by pressing the ⬆+F7 keys.

Under *Meanings* you can see which general group of **meanings** the suggestions belong to.

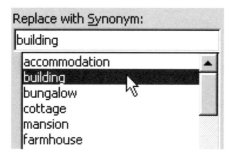

1 Choose the word 'building'.

2 Confirm via the *Replace* button.

Beware of plurals and verb forms!

The next example shows an irregular **verb form** which reads 'came', past tense of 'to come'. You can look for plurals and verb forms as follows.

The·cleaning·lady·came·

1 Position the insertion point on 'came'.

2 Start the Thesaurus with the keyboard shortcut ⇧+F7.

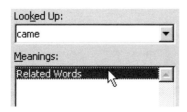

Looked Up:

came ▼

Meanings:

Related Words

3 Under *Meanings*, select the *Related Words* entry,

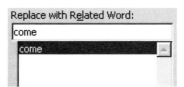

Replace with Related Word:

come

come ▲

4 then click on the highlighted entry 'come'.

109

5 Click on the *Look Up* button.

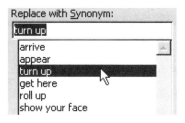

Accept the suggestion 'turn up'.

7 Confirm with a click on the *Replace* button.

As the text said 'came', you must now edit the replacement yourself and change it into 'turned up'. If you had opted for 'show your face', your personal editing efforts would have included changing 'show' to 'showed' and 'your' to 'her'.

All these tedious repetitions! Mr Grumpy still has two reccurring words in his letter: 'always' and 'problems'. Repeat the individual steps as outlined above.

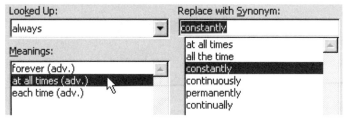

Replace the word 'always' with 'constantly'.

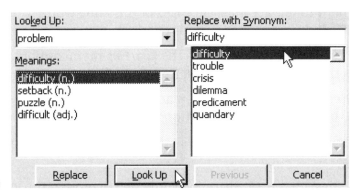

Replace the word 'problems' ...

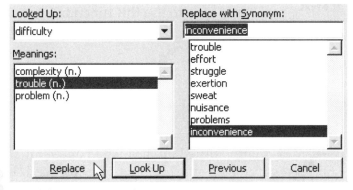

... with 'inconvenience'.

Finding and replacing text

Seek, and ye shall find. This also applies to Word. It is not unusual to use the wrong expressions while composing a letter and to wish to change words at a later date.

For example, writing a manual for the operation of a battery you may get 'plus' and 'minus' mixed up, which may have serious consequences for the reader.

Changing all the occurrences of a word in a short document is still quite manageable. However, what if the document consists of 5, 10, 50 or more pages? Would you like to scroll page by page through the whole document to replace all occurences of the same word? This may go disastrously wrong: one word is overlooked so easily.

You have two functions in Word. With the EDIT/FIND menu option, Word locates the item you are looking for.

If, on the other hand, you want to replace one expression with another, use the EDIT/REPLACE menu option.

The sample text is deliberately short, so that you can see the changes immediately.

For simplicity's sake, it is best to place the insertion point at the **beginning of the text**.

Mr Grumpy would like to replace the job title 'cleaning lady' with 'cleaning person'. Of course he could do this manually on screen, but then you would not learn how to use this function.

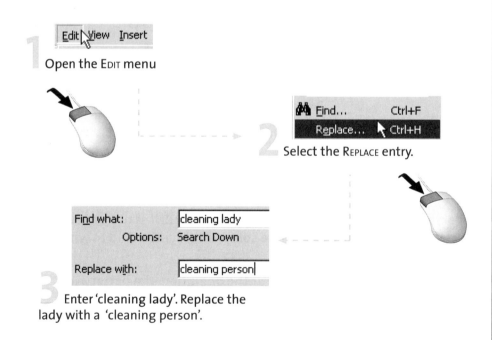

Open the EDIT menu

Select the REPLACE entry.

Enter 'cleaning lady'. Replace the lady with a 'cleaning person'.

When you select the *Replace* button, Word finds each occurrence of the item **separately**, if it is present more than once. The program always inquires whether the search is to be continued. A much quicker alternative is *Replace All*, which replaces **all occurrences** of the expression.

With the *More* button you can specify whether you want a case-sensitive search and/or whether the expression is one separate word.

At the end of the process Word tells you how many expressions have been found and replaced.

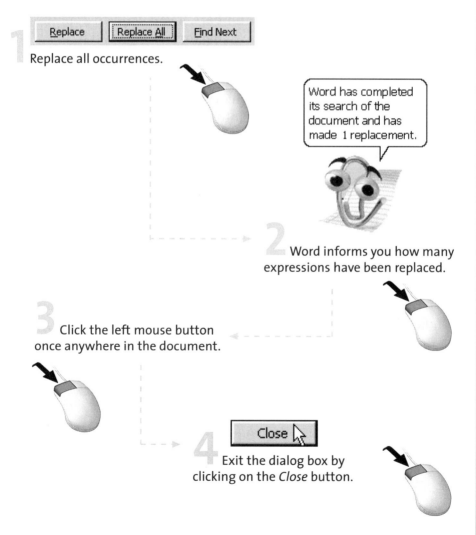

Replace all occurrences.

Word has completed its search of the document and has made 1 replacement.

2 Word informs you how many expressions have been replaced.

3 Click the left mouse button once anywhere in the document.

4 Exit the dialog box by clicking on the *Close* button.

The 'Format Painter' button

Now Mr Grumpy would like to highlight several words in bold face. You can do this individually with each word, but there is a quicker way.

It is likely that you have already noticed the button showing the **Paintbrush** and have asked yourself which function it might have.

With a single click on the Format Painter icon you can transfer formatting once. By double-clicking it you can use the function as often as you like.

You know how to highlight text or numbers. If you want to apply an **existing formatting** several times it is best to use the Format Painter button.

When you left-click on the icon, the mouse pointer changes into a paintbrush.

The function is switched off using the [Esc] key or with a second click on the button.

'Format Painter' button	Effect
Single click	You can transfer the **format once**.
Double click	You can transfer the **format any number of times**.
Pressing the [Esc] **key or clicking on the Format Painter button again**	The function is switched off.

1 The·toilets·

Position the insertion point on 'toilets'.

2 Format the word with the *Bold* button.

3 Activate the Format Painter with a double click.

1. The **toilets** were always blocked.
2. The crockery was missing from the **kitchen**.
3. The cleaning lady came only once every three days.
4. The water in the pool was far too cold.

Click on the words 'kitchen', 'cleaning lady' and 'water'.

5 Deactivate the Format Painter with the [Esc] key (you can also click once more on the button).

115

Practise, practise ... and practise again!

Exercise: lists

The members of the Beatles were:

1. John
2. Paul
3. George
4. Ringo

Type the above text and list the names of the 'Fabulous Four'.

1. John
2. Paul
3. George
4. Ringo

Select the names.

Change the list style under FORMAT/BULLETS AND NUMBERING on the *Bulleted* tab.

Drag & Drop

1 On Saturdays we visit the countryside. On Saturdays we do not have to work. On Saturdays the sun usually shines.

Type in what you are going to do on Saturday.

Mark the third sentence and move it ...

3 On Saturdays we do not have to work.

... in front of the
second one.

Exercise: finding and replacing text

1 On Saturdays we visit the countryside. On Saturdays the sun usually shines. On Saturdays we do not have to work.

Who has time to go for a drive on Saturday? Saturday is a shopping day
and Sunday is a day for visiting the countryside. Exchange the days using
Edit/Replace.

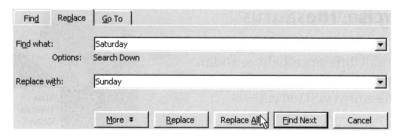

All days are to be replaced in one go.

Success: Saturday has been replaced by Sunday three times ...

On Sundays we visit the countryside. On Sundays the sun usually shines. On Sundays we do not have to work.

... and when are we going for a ride?

Exercise: Thesaurus

'Vive la différence!' What might be the 'small difference' between 'man' and 'woman'? If you don't know ... the thesaurus will tell you.

Man
Woman
Right
Ship
Murder

8 Templates and wizards

What's in this chapter:

Time is money! To save precious time, in this chapter you will learn how to create a letter template which you can use again and again. Whether you are writing a formal letter to an administrative body or sending a loving note to your friends, a personally designed letter always makes a good impression. You can speed up the process by using templates and wizards!

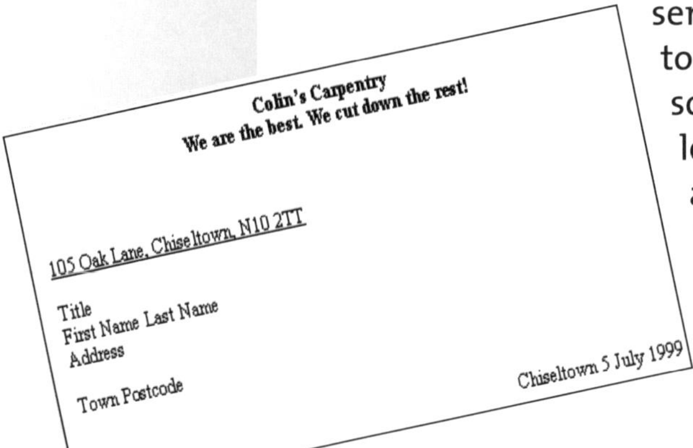

Colin's Carpentry
We are the best. We cut down the rest!

105 Oak Lane, Chiseltown, N10 2TT

Title
First Name Last Name
Address

Town Postcode

Chiseltown 5 July 1999

You already know about:

Formatting text   50
Other formatting options   53
Saving changes   69
Printing a document   76
Accessing documents   82
Creating lists   100
Moving and copying text   103
Finding and replacing text   111

You are going to learn about:

Headers and footers   122
Different views   125
Inserting a text box   126
Inserting the current date   135
Saving templates   139
Opening templates   141
Templates in Word   142
The Wizards   144

Headers and footers

A letter usually consists of the letter text. The text is the body of the letter. It also has a **head** (= header) and a **foot** (= footer). These are used to place text in the top and bottom margins of the page.

Headers and footers are displayed with the VIEW/HEADER AND FOOTER menu option.

1 Open the VIEW menu.

2 Activate the HEADER AND FOOTER entry.

The header

A new toolbar, the header and footer toolbar, appears on the screen. You will notice a dotted box. This is where you enter the text for the header.

Change the type size, choose bold lettering and centre everything.

Header
Colin's·Carpentry·Ltd¶
We·are·the·best.·We·cut·down·the·rest!¶

1 Type the text.

Header
Colin's·Carpentry·Ltd¶
We·are·the·best.·We·cut·down·the·rest!¶

2 Select the text.

14

8
9
10
11
12
14
16

3 Change the type size to '14'.

B *I* <u>U</u>

4 Click on the *Bold* button.

≡ ≡ ≡ ≡

5 Centre the whole text of the header.

123

The footer

Where there is a head, there is a foot. In most cases the footer is located at the very bottom of the page.

To illustrate this, enter your company registration information and/or VAT number here. With a mouse click on the relevant button you switch between the header and the footer.

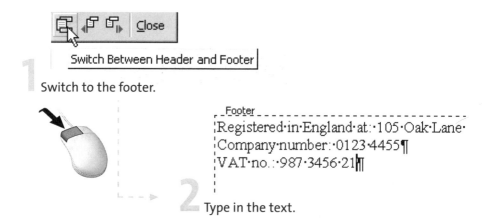

Switch to the footer.

Type in the text.

After you have entered the text, centre it and format it bold. Finish by closing the header and footer box with the *Close* button.

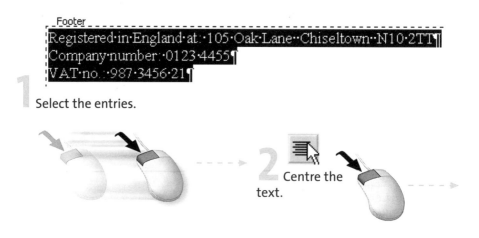

Select the entries.

Centre the text.

3 Activate the *Bold* button.

Close Header and Footer

4 Finish by clicking on the *Close* button.

Different views

In Word you can switch between various views to choose how documents are **displayed** on your screen. These options can be found in the VIEW menu.

View Insert Format
📄 Normal
🖳 Web Layout
📰 Print Layout

Layout = an alternative word for 'appearance'.

For beginners, the **Normal** and **Print Layout** views are most impor-tant. The Web Layout view is used to display a personal home page on the Internet.

Headers and footers can be viewed in the *Print Layout*.

The Print Layout is very similar to a **print-out** on paper, because here you can see the header and footer text on your screen.

View Insert

1 Click on the VIEW menu.

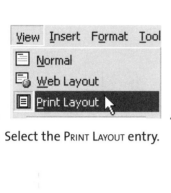

Select the PRINT LAYOUT entry.

Colin's Carpentry Ltd¶
We are the best. We cut down the rest!¶

You are now in Print Layout.

Stay in **Print Layout** view for this exercise.

If you want to return to normal view select the VIEW/NORMAL menu option.

Headers and footers are still there but they are invisible.

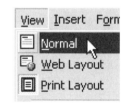

Inserting a text box

A4 standard letters are normally posted in an oblong envelope. If you use envelopes with an address window you save addressing the envelope and thus time and labour.

The addressee's name and address are placed on the letter in such a way that they can be seen through the window. First state the name of the person you are writing to.

CAUTION

For the next steps it is helpful to have **formatting characters** displayed.

Colin's·Carpentry·Ltd¶
We·are·the·best.·We·cut·down·the·rest!¶

¶
¶
¶
¶
¶
¶
¶

1 Press the ⏎ key six times.

Colin's·Carpentry·Ltd··105·Oak·Lane··Chiseltown··N10·2TI¶

2 Type in the sender. Leave two spaces between the individual entries (name, street, city).

Oak·Lane··Chiseltown·

3 It just looks a lot neater this way!

You can quickly select the whole line by placing the mouse pointer in front of it. Then, a single mouse click selects the whole line.

You can leave it at that, or format the sender's address.

To format, **select** all the data.

127

Colin's·Carpentry·Ltd··105·Oak·Lane··Chiseltown··N10·2TT¶

1 Place the mouse pointer in front of the line. Select all the sender's details with one mouse click.

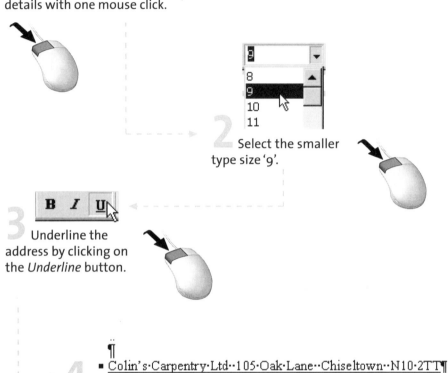

2 Select the smaller type size '9'.

3 Underline the address by clicking on the *Underline* button.

¶
■ Colin's·Carpentry·Ltd··105·Oak·Lane··Chiseltown··N10·2TT¶

4 Remove the highlighting with a click anywhere within the document.

The address box

For the address you should use a text box. Later this will have one advantage: however long the address of the recipient may be, the remainder of the text will not be moved downwards. Data entry is only carried out in the text box.

An **address box** contains
address details such as
name, street and city.

Activate the drawing
toolbar with the button
shown above.

Draw ▾ ⓇⓈ AutoShapes ▾ \ ↘ □ ○ 🖹 ◢| 🖾 ◇ ▾ ◢ ▾ A ▾ ≡ ≡ ⇄ ▣ ◍ ▾

The Drawing toolbar appears at the bottom of the screen.

To create a text box, click on the *Text Box*
button on the Drawing toolbar. The mouse
pointer changes to a cross. Move the cross below the sender's details.

Click on the
Text Box button.

Colin's·Carpentry·Ltd··105·Oak·Lane··Chiseltown··N10·2TT¶

+

Position the mouse pointer.

129

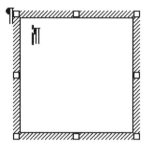

3 Click once with the left
mouse button. A **text box**
appears on the screen.

You can reposition the text box on the screen and change its size.

In this example you will specify precise
measurements in centimetres. Thus the
address/text box will fit exactly into the
address window of an envelope (provided
the paper has been folded correctly).

Place the mouse pointer precisely on the
edge of the text box, and press the right mouse button. A context
menu opens. There you will notice the *Format Text Box* item.

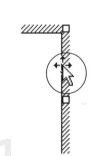

1 Place the
mouse pointer
precisely on the
edge of the
text box.

2 Press the right mouse button.
A context menu opens.

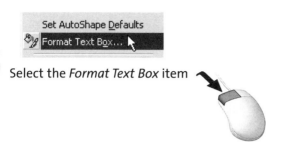

Select the *Format Text Box* item

On the *Size* tab in the dialog box, enter exactly how big (in centimetres) you want the address/text box to be.

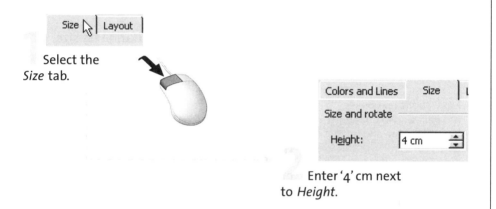

Select the *Size* tab.

Enter '4' cm next to *Height*.

Enter '8.5' cm next to *Width*.

In the next step you instruct Word at which margin you want the text box to appear. Specify *Align Left* on the *Layout* tab. In this way you place the text box on the left page margin.

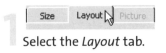

Select the *Layout* tab.

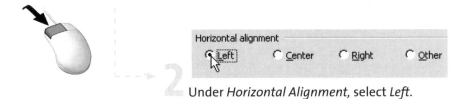

Under *Horizontal Alignment*, select *Left*.

Finally set the left internal margin to 'zero' centimetres on the *Text Box* tab. Exit the dialog box with the *OK* button.

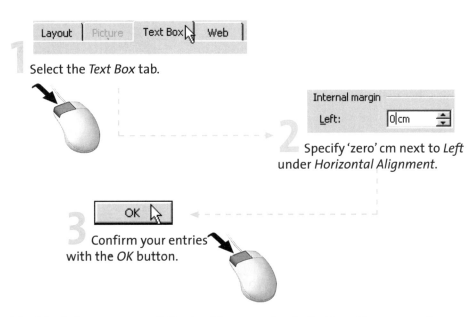

Select the *Text Box* tab.

Specify 'zero' cm next to *Left* under *Horizontal Alignment*.

Confirm your entries with the *OK* button.

The black **frame** around the text box can be irritating. To remove it use the *Line Color* button on the drawing toolbar to specify *No Line*.

One prerequisite for editing a text box is
that it is **activated**. Only then can you
edit it. The small **squares** indicate
whether it is activated or not.

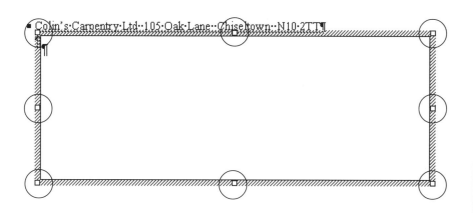

Click on the arrow next to *Line Color*.

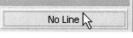

Specify *No Line*.

Next type the address details of the addressee into the text box.
Alternatively, leave the address box empty and only fill in the
necessary data when you are actually sending a letter.

As you are only preparing this letter as a **template**, in order to use it
again and again for specific letters, you can enter pseudonyms such
as 'title' (= Mr or Ms), 'first name', 'name', 'street' and 'city'.

Thus you always know that there is a text box at this place.

1 Click in the text box.

Colin's·Carpentry·Ltd··105·Oak·Lane··Chiseltown··N10·2TT¶

> Salutation¶
> First·Name·Last·Name¶
> Address¶
> ¶
> City·Post·Code¶¶

2 Enter an addressee.

You have finished with the address data. Now complete the letter.
To proceed click in the last written line before the text box.
When you press the ⏎ key the cursor automatically moves below
the text field.

Colin's·Carpentry·Ltd··105·Oak·Lane··Chiseltown··N10·2TT¶

1 Click in the line, exactly as shown
in the illustration.

- Colin's·Carpentry·Ltd··105·Oak·Lane··Chiseltown··N10·2TT¶

Salutation¶
First·Name·Last·Name¶
Address¶
¶
City·Post·Code¶

Press the ⏎ key until you can see the **cursor below the text box.**

Inserting the current date

When was the document written? With the following steps you can insert the **current date** into your document.

Press the ⏎ key twice.

Chiseltown,¶

First type the place, then add a comma and press the ⎯⎯ bar.

You now enter the date in such a way that it is automatically **updated** each time you open the document. This is achieved with the specification *Update automatically.*

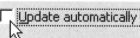

135

If you did not activate this option, the same date would always be displayed, no matter when you open the letter.

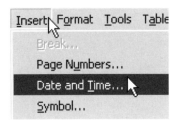

Select the INSERT/DATE AND TIME menu option.

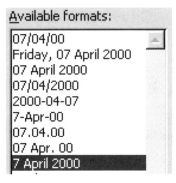

Choose a format for your date.

Activate the *Update automatically* checkbox.

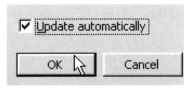

Confirm your entries with the *OK* button.

Then align your entries at the right page margin by means of the *Align Right* button.

1 Click on the *Align Right* button.

Chiseltown,·7·April·2000¶

2 The entries appear at the right margin of your document.

Chiseltown,·7·April·2000¶

3 Press the ⏎ key.

Align Left

4 Now reactivate *Align Left*. Thus you enter the remaining text from left to right.

From now on this document always displays the correct, current date at opening. No matter whether you open it tomorrow, next week, next year, or next century: Word continually updates it. (Provided your computer keeps track of the time, of course!)

The times they are a-changin'

Your computer should always be current with regard to date and time. As a user of Windows 95, 98 or Windows NT you are always informed about what time it is. The time is displayed on the **taskbar.**

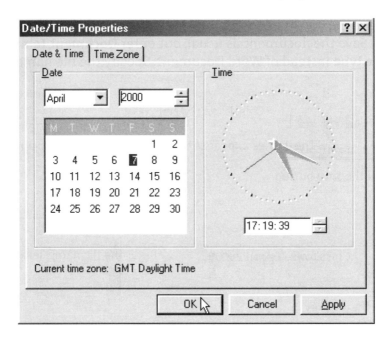

However, if your computer is not connected to a radio clock or to an Internet time service, there is of course no guarantee that the displayed time and date are correct. Point the mouse to the clock on the taskbar and double-click on it. On the *Date and Time* tab you can set the correct date and time.

TIP

Windows 95 and 98 automatically adjust the clock to take account of **daylight saving changes.**

Saving templates

You want to be able to reuse your letter template again and again. However, you need not enter the header and the footer, the address box or the date every time you do so.

Simply save the document as a **template** and open it whenever required. Save the document as usual, but enter **Document Template** as the **file type** instead of Word Document. Specify the file name as 'letter'.

Click on the *Save* button.

File name: | Letter

Enter the file name 'letter'.

Save as type: | Word Document (*.doc)

Click on the arrow on the right-hand side to view a list of options for the file type.

In Word, the file names of templates end in **.dot**.

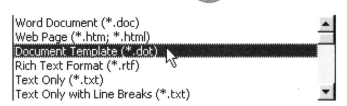

Word Document (*.doc)
Web Page (*.htm; *.html)
Document Template (*.dot)
Rich Text Format (*.rtf)
Text Only (*.txt)
Text Only with Line Breaks (*.txt)

Select the entry *Document Template (*.dot)*.

Word keeps a separate **folder for templates**. Whenever you *specify Document Template* as file type, Word automatically 'jumps' to this directory.

Save in:
Templates

Save in:
Letters & Faxes

TheTemplates folder is in turn divided into separate areas, similar to a ring-binder with different tabs.

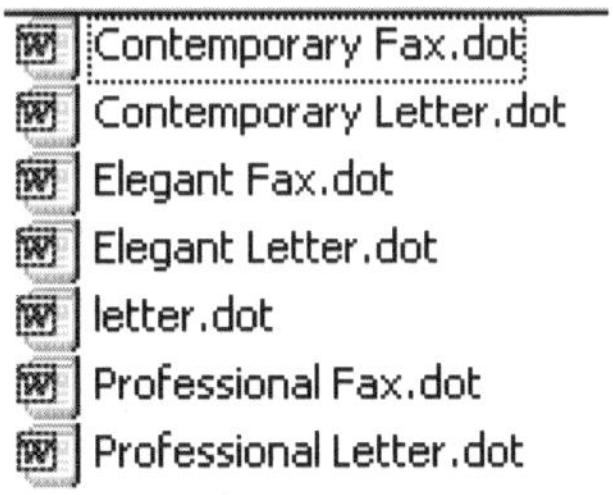
Contemporary Fax.dot
Contemporary Letter.dot
Elegant Fax.dot
Elegant Letter.dot
letter.dot
Professional Fax.dot
Professional Letter.dot

For this letter, the *Letters & Faxes* folder seems to be appropriate.

Word templates for various letters and faxes are stored here (more on this topic later in this chapter).

Letters & Faxes

1 Save the template in the *Letters & Faxes* folder.

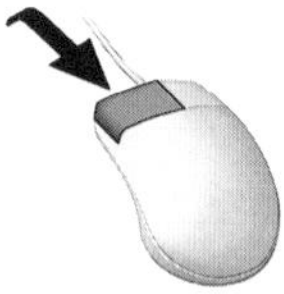

Save

2 Save the document template with a click on the *Save* button.

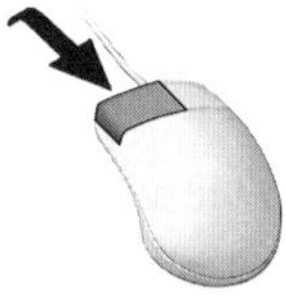

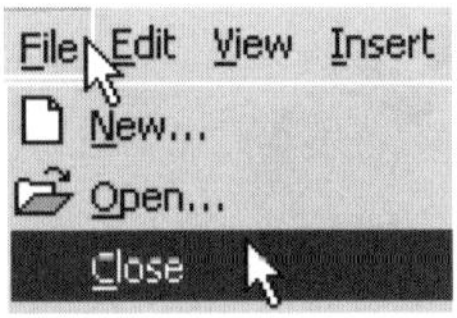
File
Edit
View
Insert
New...
Open...
Close

3 Close the document template via the FILE/CLOSE menu option.

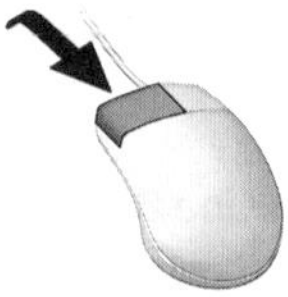

Opening templates

You already know how to create a new document. There are two ways of doing this. The first is to click on the *New* button. Word immediately creates a new document on the screen.

The second way leads you via the menu. The menu option FILE/NEW opens the *New* dialog box.

For the 'Letter' template, simply select the tab (in this case the *Letters & Faxes* folder) in which you previously saved it.

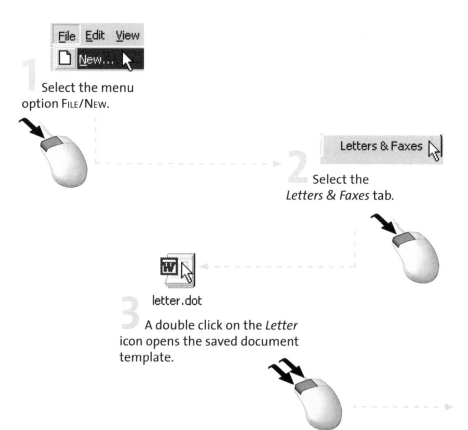

1 Select the menu option FILE/NEW.

2 Select the *Letters & Faxes* tab.

letter.dot

3 A double click on the *Letter* icon opens the saved document template.

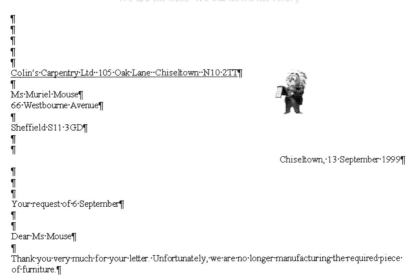

Colin's·Carpentry·Ltd¶
We·are·the·best.·We·cut·down·the·rest!¶

¶
¶
¶
¶
Colin's·Carpentry·Ltd··105·Oak·Lane··Chiseltown··N10·2TT¶
¶
Ms·Muriel·Mouse¶
66·Westbourne·Avenue¶
¶
Sheffield·S11·3GD¶
¶
¶

Chiseltown,·13·September·1999¶

¶
¶
¶
Your·request·of·6·September¶
¶
¶
Dear·Ms·Mouse¶
¶
Thank·you·very·much·for·your·letter.·Unfortunately,·we·are·no·longer·manufacturing·the required·piece·
of·furniture.¶

Now you only need to enter the appropriate text. If you want to
keep a specific letter, simply save it as a normal document under
a separate file name.

Templates in Word

Document templates are forms for the creation of documents.

Select one of the tabs in the *New* dialog box.
You recognise the standard letters which
are called **document templates**.

They contain suggestions which you may or may
not adopt. The names are associative, so you can
guess what the templates are likely to contain.

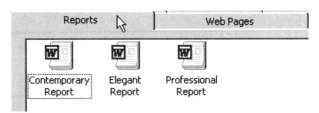

You can adopt, modify and personalise the suggestions.

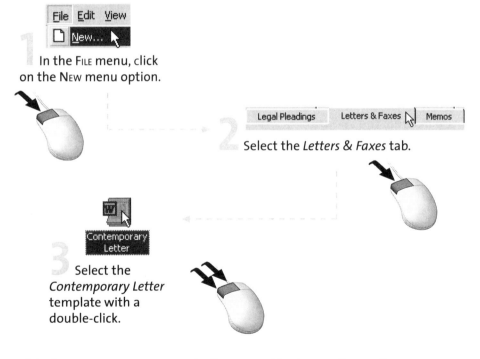

In the FILE menu, click on the NEW menu option.

Select the *Letters & Faxes* tab.

Select the *Contemporary Letter* template with a double-click.

This does **not** open an **empty document** but a **ready-made text**. On the title bar you will see the ending '.dot' instead of the usual '.doc'.

This means that you are not working with a document but with a template. Simply overtype the suggestions with your own data.

The Wizards

Apart from the above templates, Word also provides Wizards. These can spare you many a tedious task.

Word offers you help in creating letters and faxes (on the *Letters & Faxes* tab). Furthermore it also assists you in writing your CV.

On the *Other Documents* tab you can find the **Resume Wizard** (which will actually open the **CV Wizard** dialog).

Step by step, the Wizard directs you to your goal. You activate it by double-clicking on the icon.

Agenda Wizard   Batch Conversi...   Calendar Wizard   Contemporary Resume

Elegant Resume   Professional Resume   Resume Wizard

1 Select the FILE/NEW menu option.

Other Documents

2 Select the *Other Documents* tab.

Start the Wizard
with a double-click.

The **Resume Wizard**
(**CV Wizard**) appears
on the screen. In the
left-hand column you
can see small boxes.
They indicate your
current location in
the Wizard.
If you click on a
different point you
will skip the ones in
between.

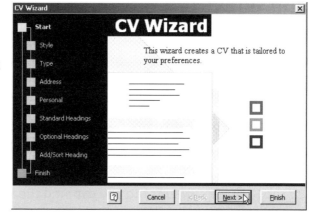

Use the *Next* button at the bottom of the dialog box to move onto
the next form.

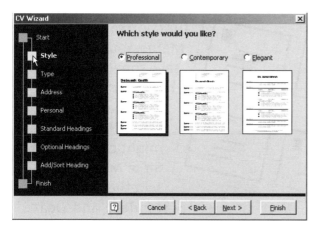

You will proceed
step by step. Your
specifications are
entered in the right
half. These are mostly
carried out with
mouse clicks.

145

What's in this chapter:

When you are sending the same letter to several addresses, you do not have to insert each address manually. You can do something else instead. Word contains a function called Mail Merge. You can save time and labour by integrating the salutation in your letter. Thus, you might choose 'Dear Sir or Madam', together with 'Yours sincerely' as standard, and 'Dear ...' and 'Love and kisses' as an alternative. You will also find out about how to switch between these formulations depending on the addressee.

You already know about:

Formatting text   50
Other formatting options   53
Saving changes   69
Printing a document   76
Finding and replacing text   111
Headers and footers   122
Saving templates   139
Templates in Word   142
The Wizards   144

You are going to learn about:

What is Mail Merge?   148
Creating a form letter   149
The data source   151
Field names   151
Saving data sources   155
Editing data sources   157
Inserting merge fields   160
The salutation   164
If ... then ... else ...   165
Merging a data source with a form letter   170

What is Mail Merge?

Letters such as invitations are often sent to several people at the same time.

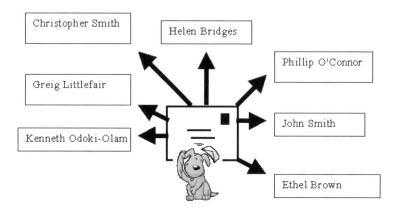

You do not have to write the letter all over again: in Word you can use the Mail Merge function instead. In this way you do not have to insert an address and salutation in each letter.

A **Mail Merge** form letter consists of two components:
1. the **letter text** which always remains the same
2. the **data** which is different for each individual address.

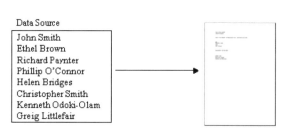

You enter the address details (name, street, city, and so on) in a separate file, called a **data source**, and **merge** it with the main document.

Creating a form letter

To instruct Word to **create a form letter** you have to activate the menu item TOOLS and then click on the MAIL MERGE entry.

Open the
TOOLS menu.

Select the MAIL MERGE
command.

The **Mail Merge Helper**
opens. As you want to create
a mail merge document, click
on the *Create* button next to
the number *1* and select the
Form Letters item.

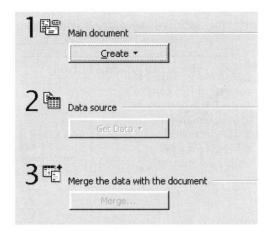

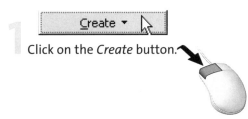

Click on the *Create* button.

149

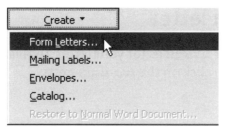

Select the *Mail Merge* function.

Word asks you whether you would like to use the active window or create a new main document. **Active window** means that you are referring to the document which is currently opened on your screen. The *New Main Document* command creates a new document.

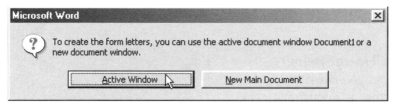

Select the *Active Window* button.

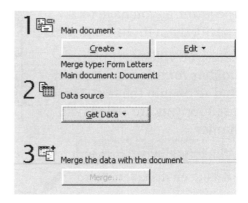

The Mail Merge helper reappears on your screen.

The data source

You still have to enter the addresses for your letter: that is, you have to create a **data source**.

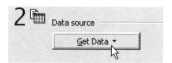

Under *Data Source* click on the *Get Data* button.

Activate the *Create Data Source* button.

Field names

In the next step a number of items will be chosen for the planned form letter. You have to decide which fields you require to be in the letter, as you have to specify them in the next step.

Later you will insert place-holders for title, name, street, and so on into the text. These pseudonyms are called **field names**.

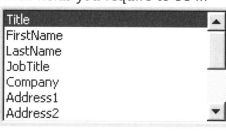

Which field names do you need for this letter?

General	Example
Title	Mr
First name	John
Last name	Smith
Street	13 The Headrow
City	Leeds
Postcode	LS1 7XY

Deleting field names

Word usually provides **too many** field names. Details such as 'Position' or 'Address2' can be **removed** from the list in this example. To delete items, first click on the name, and then on the *Remove Field Name* button.

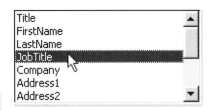

Click on the field name 'Position'.

Activate the *Remove Field Name* button.

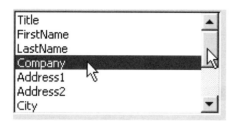

Remove the entries 'Company, Address1, Address2, State, Country, HomePhone, WorkPhone'.

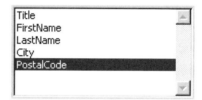

The list should now look like this.

Inserting field names

Via the *Add Field Names* button you can insert **new field names**. Here, add the field name 'Street'.

Field name:
| Street |

Enter 'Street' as a new field name.

Confirm your entry with the *Add Field Name* button.

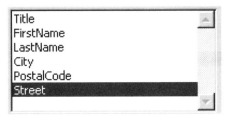

The new field name has been added to the list.

Sorting field names

The order of entries (title, first name, last name, street, city, postcode) should be the same as the order of their appearance in the letter.

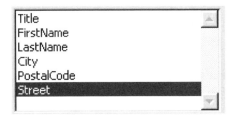

«Title»
«FirstName» «LastName»
«Street»

«City» «PostalCode»

The correct order of entries makes merging letters much easier. With the aid of the **Move arrows** you can modify your list accordingly.

Move

Modify the order of the field names, ...

2 ... until the list looks like this.

3 Confirm your changes with the *OK* button.

Saving data sources

To make it possible for you to use the address database (the entire address collection), which you are going to create, for other form letters, you have to **save** it.

Try to use **'associative' names** (such as customers, suppliers, relatives) to make it immediately obvious which data is contained in which database. In this example, use the name 'Addresses'.

1 Specify 'Addresses' as the file name.

2 Save the file.

155

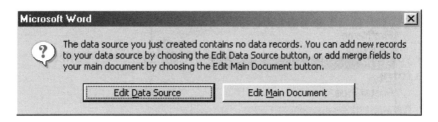

Word notifies you that the data source – the address database – still has to be compiled. You have not yet entered any data.

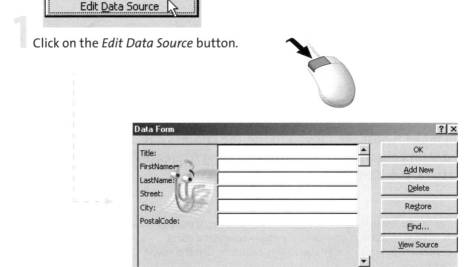

1 Click on the *Edit Data Source* button.

2 You are now entering the next phase: inputting the data into the source.

Editing data sources

Now you can start to enter data for individuals in the **opened data form**.

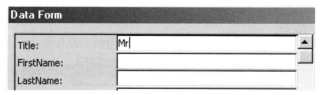

Enter the first record.

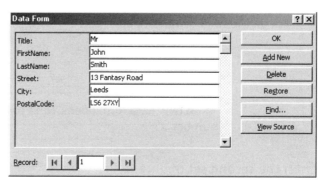

Enter the details into the appropriate boxes:
Mr
John
Smith
13 Fantasy Road
Leeds
LS6 7XY

Once you have completed your first record, activate the *Add New* button.

In this example, one **record** consists of the details of one person. These details may be first name, last name, city, and so on.

Click on the *Add New* button.

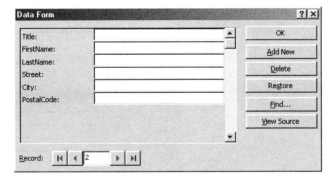

A new data form opens. Next to Record you will see the number '2'.

Enter the **second** set of data.

To simplify the exercise, only two addressees are listed. This is enough to explain the mail merge function. However, use the addresses of one male and one female person.

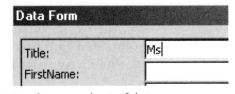

Enter the second set of data.

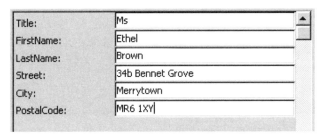

Title:	Ms
FirstName:	Ethel
LastName:	Brown
Street:	34b Bennet Grove
City:	Merrytown
PostalCode:	MR6 1XY

2 Input the details into the appropriate boxes:

Ms
Ethel
Brown
34b Bennet Grove
Merrytown
MR6 1XY

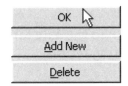

1 Once you have entered all addresses, **leave** the data form by pressing the *OK* button.

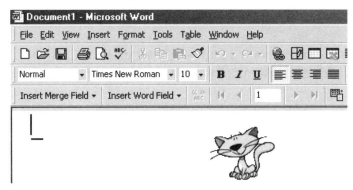

2 This returns you to your document.

159

Inserting merge fields

After you have left the data form via the OK button, you return to your document.

You will notice a new toolbar with various mail merge functions on your screen.

How do you return to the data form?

By clicking on the *Mail Merge Helper* button on the new toolbar you return to the Mail Merge Helper.

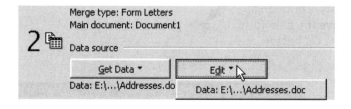

Mail Merge Helper

Activate the *Edit* button under *Data Source*, and click on the **data source document** (here **Addresses.doc**). You return to the data form, for example, to create new records or to edit existing records.

Merge type: Form Letters
Main document: Document1

2 Data source

Get Data ▾   Edit ▾

Data: E:\...\Addresses.do   Data: E:\...\Addresses.doc

Back to the main document 'Invitation'. You still need to specify the **fields** and their position within the letter.

Joe Bloggs¶
123 Fiction Road¶
Sheffield¶
S34 3RG¶

First enter the sender.

Joe·Bloggs¶
123·Fiction·Road¶
Sheffield¶
S34·3RG¶
¶
¶
¶
¶
¶
¶

It looks like you're
writing a letter.

Would you like help?

● Get help with
   writing the letter

● Just type the
   letter without
   help

[Cancel]

Press the ⏎ key six times.

Position the cursor exactly
where you want to have the
first field (here: 'Title').

If the Assistant offers
you help, decline it.

In the mail merge toolbar, activate *Insert Merge Field*.

Sheffield¶
S34·3RG¶
¶
¶
¶
¶
¶
¶

Position the cursor exactly
five lines below the sender.

161

Joe·Bloggs¶
123·Fiction·Road¶
Sheffield¶
S34·3RG¶

2 Click on the *Insert Merge Field* button.

Select the first field (here 'Title') from the submenu.

1 Click on the *Title* entry.

«Title»¶

2 The merge field has been inserted.

«Title»¶
▯

3 Press the ⏎ key once.

4 Specify the *FirstName* entry.

«FirstName»·¶

5 Press the ⬜ bar.

6 Activate the *LastName* entry.

If you adopt the empty lines as outlined in the above steps, your letter will fit into the envelope with the address visible in the envelope window (provided the letter has been folded correctly).

Insert the remaining **merge fields** (FirstName, LastName, Street, City, Postcode) in the correct **order** in the address field.

1 Enter the fields ' Street, City, and Postcode' ...

«Title»¶
«FirstName»·«LastName»¶
«Street»¶
«City»¶
«PostCode»¶

2 ... in the correct order into the text.

Field codes – yes or no?

A crucial point for the **appearance** of your field in the document is whether the *Field Codes* option on the *View* tab in the TOOLS/OPTIONS menu option is active.

If View is **switched on** the 'Title' field appears as shown on the right.

If, on the other hand, the option is **deactivated** the field looks different, as shown below.

«Title»¶
«FirstName»·«LastName»¶   ☐ Field codes
«Street»¶
«City»¶
«PostCode»¶

MERGEFIELD·Title·¶
MERGEFIELD·FirstName·¶MERGEFIELD·LastName·¶   ☑ Field codes
MERGEFIELD·Street·¶
MERGEFIELD·City·¶
MERGEFIELD·PostCode·¶

It does not matter which appearance you choose as the mail merge procedure is not affected by it.

The salutation

Since the same text will not be sent to every addressee, the first item to be considered is the **salutation**. This can be anything, from the rather formal 'Dear Sir or Madam', closing with 'Yours sincerely' to 'Dear ...', followed by 'Love and kisses'.

Moreover, if you write to partners in other European countries, things are different again, and the whole salutation changes with the sex of the person (Caro signor/Cara signora/Lieber Herr/Liebe Frau/Chère Madame/Cher Monsieur to name just a few).

Chère Madame Dupont
Lieber Herr Mayer
Cara Signora Cinquetti

However, you can save yourself a lot of typing, and not include the actual salutation in the data form at all.

A woman should be addressed as 'Dear Ms ...', a man as 'Dear Mr ...', while a letter addressed to 'Messrs ...' requires 'Dear Sirs' and an anonymous partner is properly addressed as 'Dear Sir or Madam'.

You can replace the **introduction** with anything you like, such as Dear Name or any other introduction suitable for your letter. Remember never to put a comma after the introductory salutation and to start the first word with an upper case letter.

You can replace the **closing formula** with anything you like, such as Yours faithfully, or any other salutation suitable for your letter. Remember that Yours is always upper case, while faithfully or sincerely is always lower case and never followed by a punctuation mark.

If ... then ... else ...

The If ... then ... else ... option can be used to address your mail merge letters to either a man or a woman.

If ...

If you are not addressing a woman, then the program assumes you are addressing a man. There is no in between (for the software).

Condition	Condition does not apply
Man	Woman
Hearing	Deaf
Seeing	Blind
Dead	Alive
On	Off

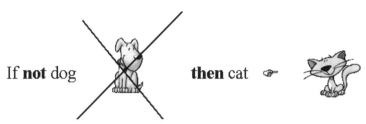

If **not** dog   **then** cat   ☞

Is there a criterion with which Word can decide whether the named person is a man or a woman? Yes, and it is the'Title' **field** in the address database. The field is structured differently depending on what sex the named person is.

Sex	Difference
Female	**Data Form** Title: `Ms` FirstName: `Stefania`
Male	**Data Form** Title: `Mr` FirstName: `John`

Insert Word Field ⏷

Click on the *Insert Word Field* button.

Activate the *If ... then ... else...* entry.

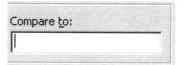

Click into the *Compare to* field.

Type in 'Mr'.

Sex	Effect in the salutation			
Female	Dear Ms ... Dear Madam	Chère Madame	Cara Signora
Male	Dear Mr ... Dear Sir	Cher Monsieur	Caro Signore

then ...

If the field contains the *Title* 'Mr',
Word should execute the instruction
'Dear Sir'.

Dear Sir

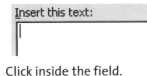

1 Click inside the field.

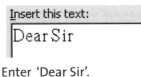

2 Enter 'Dear Sir'.

else ...

If the title is not 'Mr', the salutation
should read 'Dear Madam'.

Dear Madam

1 Click inside the field.

Please note that the text
you enter in the **then...**
else... fields may extend
over several lines.

Otherwise insert this text:
Dear Madam

2 Type your required salutation.

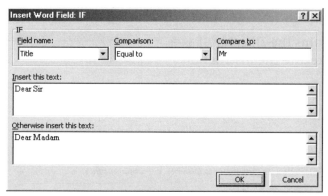

Confirm by clicking on the *OK* button.

You return to the document and now the salutation reads 'Dear Sir'.

This expression is displayed because you have chosen a salutation without the recipient's name.

«Title»
«FirstName» «LastName»
«Street»
«City», «PostalCode»

If in the salutation the recipients are to be addressed using their last name, you insert the 'Title' field, then you complete the salutation by first pressing the ⬚ bar to insert a gap and finally inserting the merge field 'LastName'.

Dear «Title» «LastName»

Dear Mr ¶

Insert a space by pressing the ⬚ bar.

Insert the *LastName* merge field...

169

Dear Mr·«Name»¶

3 ... into the document.

Dear·Mr·<<LastNames>>¶
¶
Thank·you·very·much·for·your·kind·letter·wishing·us·success·in·our·new·venture.¶
¶
Looking·forward·to·working·with·you.¶
¶
Best·regards¶
¶
¶
Joe·Bloggs¶

4 Complete the letter.

Merging a data source with a form letter

Via the *View Merged Data* button you can **preview** your form letters on your screen.

1 Click on the *View Merged Data* button.

2 Also preview the second record.

If you click on the button *View Merged Data* a second time you return to the main document.

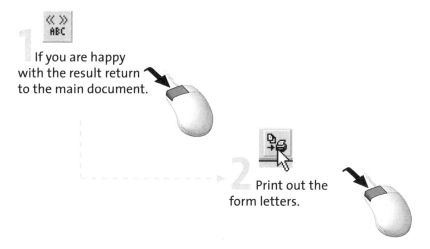

If you are happy with the result return to the main document.

Print out the form letters.

Exiting Word and saving

When you **exit** Word you will be asked whether you want to **save** the changes in the document and the address database. Confirm with *Yes*.

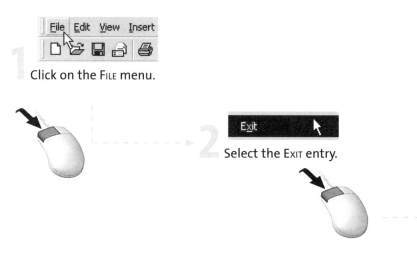

Click on the FILE menu.

Select the EXIT entry.

171

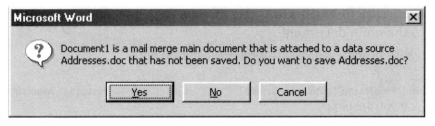

Microsoft Word ✕

? Document1 is a mail merge main document that is attached to a data source Addresses.doc that has not been saved. Do you want to save Addresses.doc?

Yes | No | Cancel

3 Confirm with *Yes*.

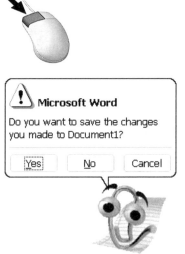

⚠ **Microsoft Word**

Do you want to save the changes you made to Document1?

Yes | No | Cancel

4 Click on *Yes* again. Use 'FormLetter' as the file name.

Practise, practise ... and practise again!

Create an address database with the following data:

Title	FirstName	LastName	Street	City	Postcode	Amount	D/O
Mr	Peter	Jones	66 Hull Street	Sheffield	S1 2XY	250	D
Mr	John	Foreman	15 York Road	Leeds	LS3 4ZX	450	O
Ms	Sharon	Edwards	45 Otley Road	Birmingham	B5 6XY	890	O
Mr	Fred	Morley	1 Park Lane	London	SW7 8ZX	300	D
Mr	Brian	Tate	7 Church Grove	Birmingham	B9 1XY	120	O
Ms	Maria	Fernando	88 Castle Hill	Sheffield	S2 3ZX	450	D

Create a form letter! Solve the First/Last reminder and the due/
overdue problems elegantly by using *If ... then ... else ...*

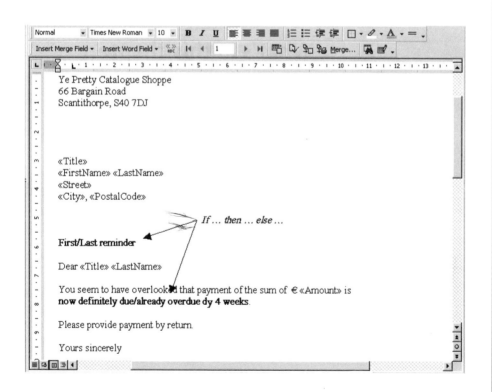

What's in this chapter:

Letters such as job applications often contain identical phrases. You can save time and effort by creating them once, and then inserting them whenever required. This chapter is all about 'Autos': AutoComplete, AutoText, and AutoCorrect.

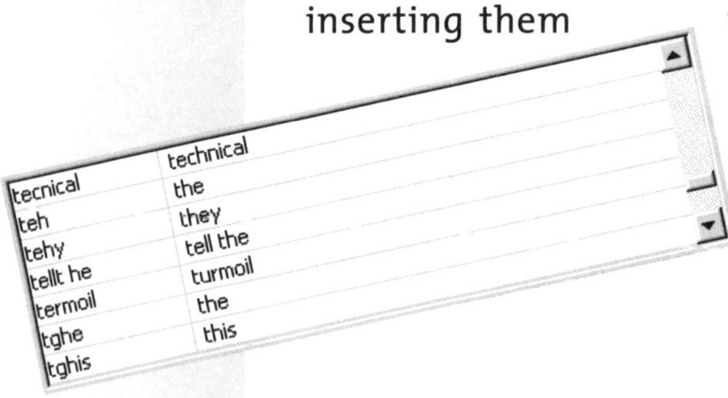

tecnical	technical
teh	the
tehy	they
tellt he	tell the
termoil	turmoil
tghe	the
tghis	this

You already know about:

The Word spelling checker 40
Formatting text 50
Other formatting options 53
Saving changes 69
Saving to diskette 72
Moving and copying text 103
The Thesaurus 106
Finding and replacing text 111
Saving templates 139
The Wizards 144
Creating a form letter 149

You are going to learn about:

AutoComplete 176
AutoText and AutoCorrect 179
Creating AutoText 179
Inserting AutoText 181
AutoCorrect 183
Using AutoText, AutoCorrect and
  tips in letters 185

AutoComplete

Perhaps you have already noticed that while you are typing, Word offers you a **suggestion** from time to time. This is particularly obvious when you are writing the days of the week. For example, when you type 'Mond', the program offers you 'Monday'.

Monday	Tuesday	Wednesday
Mond	Tues	Wedn

January	February	August
Janu	Febr	Augu

WHAT'S THIS?

The words in the yellow boxes are called '**tips**'.

You can accept a tip by pressing the ⏎ key. This works for all **days of the week**. The function is also available for longer names of **months**, like January, February, and August. When you write the **current date**, a tip is displayed too.

Other words have also already been filed. You can find these items on the *AutoText* tab in the Tools/ AutoCorrect menu option.

tecnical	technical	
teh	the	
tehy	they	
tellt he	tell the	
termoil	turmoil	
tghe	the	
tghis	this	

Here you can also create expressions, for example your name or longer words (for example 'extraordinarily'). You thus only have to type these expressions once, and then save them.

In this example enter 'Thomas Whatsisname'. You can either type the name in the document and select it, or enter it into the dialog box later.

Thomas Whatsisname
Thom

→ Thomas Whatsisname

1 Select the TOOLS/ AUTOCORRECT menu option.

2 Select the *AutoText* tab.

Show AutoComplete tip for AutoText and dates
To accept the AutoComplete tip, press Enter

3 Tick the checkbox if necessary.

Enter AutoText entries here:
Thomas Whatsisname

4 Enter 'Thomas Whatsisname'.

Add

Delete

5 Click on the *Add* button.

OK

6 Confirm your entries with the *OK* button.

177

Deleting tips

You can delete a tip in the dialog box by first clicking on the tip and then on the *Delete* button.

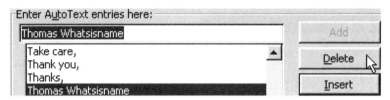

Inserting tips

After you have created 'Thomas Whatsisname' as a tip, type the name. When you press the ⏎ key, Word accepts the complete name and inserts it at this point.

If you do **not want to accept** a tip just continue writing.

> Thomas Whatsisname
> Thom|

1 Write 'Thom'.

> Thomas·Whatsisname¶

2 Accept the tip by pressing the ⏎ key.

> Thomas·Whatsisname¶
> 123·Bridge·Lane¶
> Bromley¶
> BR2·5QS¶
> ¶
> ¶
> ¶
> ¶
> ¶
> ¶

3 Complete the address and press the ⏎ key six times.

AutoText and AutoCorrect

In Word 2000 you can enter **phrases** or **text passages** once and **insert** them into documents whenever required. You have two options.

AutoText

You save text and give it a name. As soon as you write this name and press the F3 key, Word inserts the saved text.

AutoCorrect

This option was originally designed for the purpose of you entering mistakes you frequently make so that Word can correct them automatically (for example 'teh' instead of 'the').

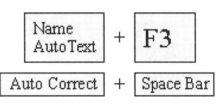

However, you can change this function a little: you can also file and name **text passages**. Subsequently, whenever you write one of the names and press the [   ] bar. Word automatically inserts the saved text.

Which function should I choose: AutoText or AutoCorrect?

This entirely depends on you and is a matter of taste.
In practice, **text passages** are usually made up using **AutoText.**

Creating AutoText

In this example you first create a sender's address as AutoText. Assign it the name 'sdr'.

If you know how many empty lines have to follow the last line of the sender's address, enter these too. In this way the cursor will always jump to the correct position.

Thomas·Whatsisname¶
123·Bridge·Lane¶
Bromley¶
BR2·5QS¶
¶
¶
¶
¶
¶

1 Select the shown text passage including the empty lines.

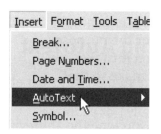

Insert	Format	Tools	Table

Break...
Page Numbers...
Date and Time...
AutoText ▶
Symbol...

2 Select the INSERT/AUTOTEXT menu option.

New... ▶ Alt+F3

3 Click on the NEW entry.

Create AutoText ? X

Word will create an AutoText entry from the current selection.

Please name your AutoText entry:

Thomas Whatsisname

| OK | Cancel |

4 Word suggests a name, but you may replace it with a shorter one.

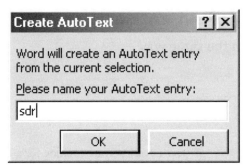

5 Enter the abbreviation 'sdr',
and confirm it using the *OK* button.

Inserting AutoText

You have created an AutoText entry. The complete data for Thomas
Whatsisname is **saved** under the name 'sdr'.

As soon as you type the abbreviation 'sdr' and press the ⒡⒊ key,
Word inserts the whole text (including the empty lines selected
in step 1).

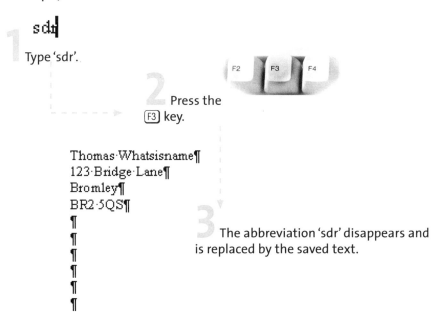

1 Type 'sdr'.

2 Press the
⒡⒊ key.

3 The abbreviation 'sdr' disappears and
is replaced by the saved text.

181

Creating several AutoText entries

Create more text passages in the same way.

1 Your job offer in the│

Enter the text under the name 're'.

2 in your advert you are looking for a ...

Assign the name 'Text1'.

3 I have read your job offer with great interest.

Save the AutoText under 'Text2'.

4 I have been a sales executive for rubber hoses. To keep my knowledge up-to-date I took an Open University course for two years.

Enter 'Text3'.

5 I have been a sales executive for rubber hoses. To keep my knowledge up-to-date I took an Open University course for two years.

This passage is filed as 'Text4'.

6 Unfortunately, my job was taken over by a computer.

Use the name 'Text5'.

7 I would like to discuss further details in an interview.

Save the text passage as AutoText under the name 'Text6'.

AutoCorrect

Abbreviations shorten your entries! AutoCorrect is best used for **phrases** or **abbreviations**.

An example: you always read the Times Educational Supplement, or for short TES. Here you find a job ad which you want to reply to. In your letter you refer to the paper. Enter the abbreviation 'TES' for 'Times Educational Supplement' in AutoCorrect.

In AutoCorrect it does not matter whether you first write the text and select it or enter it into the dialog box later on.

Times Educational Supplement

Type 'Times Educational Supplement'.

Select the entry.

Select the Tools/AutoCorrect menu option.

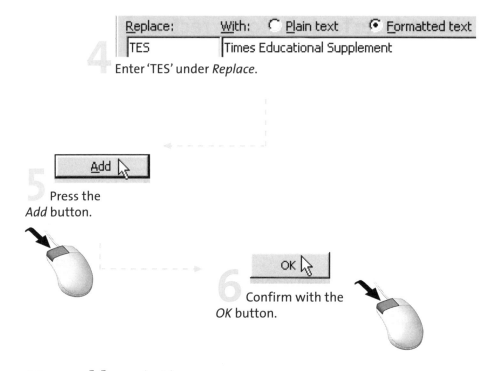

| Replace: | With: | ○ Plain text | ● Formatted text |

| TES | Times Educational Supplement |

Enter 'TES' under *Replace*.

5 Press the *Add* button.

6 Confirm with the *OK* button.

More abbreviations ...

Since you probably read more than one newspaper, you can create further abbreviations in AutoCorrect. The papers are the Yorkshire Post and the Glasgow Herald.

Save the following details in AutoCorrect, as you have been shown.

1 Yorkshire Post

Specify the name 'YP'.

2 Glasgow Herald

Assign the name 'GH'.

Using AutoText, AutoCorrect and tips in letters

You would be surprised how fast you can write a letter once you have saved everything.

First, create a **new document**. First enter the abbreviation 'sdr' and press the F3 key. Word automatically inserts the sender Thomas Whatsisname and the empty lines.

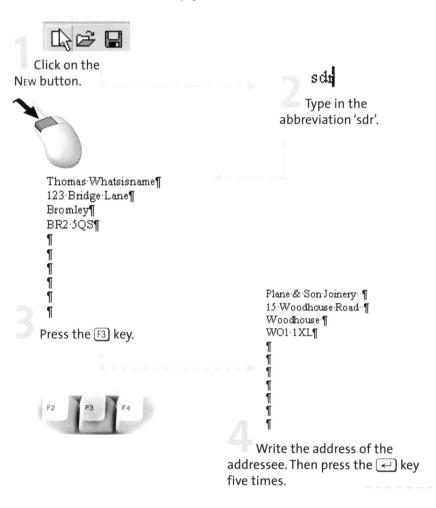

Click on the
NEW button.

Type in the
abbreviation 'sdr'.

Thomas·Whatsisname¶
123·Bridge·Lane¶
Bromley¶
BR2·5QS¶
¶
¶
¶
¶
¶
¶

Press the F3 key.

Plane·&·Son·Joinery···¶
15·Woodhouse·Road··¶
Woodhouse·¶
WO1·1XL¶
¶
¶
¶
¶
¶
¶

Write the address of the
addressee. Then press the ↵ key
five times.

185

RE:¶

5 Enter 'RE:'.

Your job offer in the|

6 Press the F3 key.

The job ad appeared in the Times Educational Supplement. It is filed under the abbreviation 'TES' in AutoCorrect.

Your·job·offer·in·the·TES¶

1 Type 'TES'.

Your·job·offer·in·the·Times·Educational·Supplement¶

2 Press the ⬚ bar.

Your·job·offer·in·the·Times·Educational·Supplement¶
¶
¶
¶

3 Press the ⏎ key three times.

The salutation 'Dear Sir or Madam' is inserted here.

The abbreviation 'Dsom' already exists in AutoCorrect.

1 Dsom¶

Type 'Dsom'.

2 Dear·Sir·or·Madam¶

Press the ⬚ key.

Now there follow a number of text passages. Enter their names and press the F3 key.

1 Dear·Sir·or·Madam¶
¶
I·have·read·your·job·offer·with·great·interest.¶

Type 'Text2'. Press the F3 key.

2 Dear·Sir·or·Madam¶
¶
I·have·read·your·job·offer·with·great·interest.¶
¶
The·job·you·are·offering·has·immediately·caught·my·interest.·I·am· currently·looking·for·a·new·professional·challenge.¶
¶

Type 'Text3'. Press the F3 key.

3 Dear Sir or Madam   Alt + F3

I have read your job offer with great interest. The job you are offering immediately caught my attention I am currently looking for a new professional challenge.

For two years I have been a sale executive for rubber house. To keep my knowledge up-to-date I took an Open University Course.

Write 'Text4'. Press the F3 key.

187

Dear·Sir·or·Madam¶
¶
I·have·read·your·job·offer·with·great·interest.·¶
¶
The·job·you·are·offering·immediately·caught·my·attention.·I·am·currently·looking·for·a·new·professional·challenge.¶
¶
For·two·years·I·have·been·a·sale·executive·for·rubber·house.·To·keep·my·knowledge·up-to-date·I·took·an·Open·University·Course.¶
¶
I·would·like·to·discuss·further·details·in·person.¶
¶

4 Write 'Text6'. Press the ⒡₃ key.

At the end of the letter type 'ys' and press the ⬜ bar.
This will turn into 'Yours sincerely,'.

The abbreviation
'ys' already exists
in AutoCorrect.

I·would·like·to·discuss·further·details·in·person.¶
¶
ys¶

1 Type ' ys '.

Yours sincerely

2 Press the ⬜ key.

After the greeting, Thomas Whatsisname signs the letter. In this case this means that the name is repeated.

Yours·sincerely·¶
¶
¶
Thomas Whatsisname
Thom¶

1 Write 'Thom'.

Thomas·Whatsisname

2 Accept 'Thomas Whatsisname' by pressing the ⏎ key.

Practise, practise ... and practise again!

Create the following AutoText entries:

Text	Name of AutoText
The Treadmill 111 Walker Lane Dronfield S30 4SH	send
Your application of ... Your application note of ... Your telephone enquiry	a1 a2 a3
Dear Mr ... Dear Ms ...	title1 title2
Thank you for your interest in our enterprise.	tex1
Please send a copy of curriculum vitae.	tex2
We would like to invite you for an interview.	tex3
Sorry, the vacancy has been filled.	tex4
We wish you all the best for your future career.	tex5

With the AutoText entries created above, write the following letters to the three individuals. Insert the missing details.

1. Peter Swashbuckle, 21 Success Rise, Rotherham S40 1JS, a2, 2 Feb, title1, tex1, tex2, ys
2. Rosa Innocenti, 66 Cloister Close, Chapeltown S27 6HH, a1, 1 Feb, title2, tex1, tex3, 17 Mar, ys
3. Fred Busibody, 41 Toiler's Crescent, Attercliffe S9 3HQ, a1, 3 Feb, title1, tex1, tex4, tex5, ys

What's in this chapter:

Whether at Easter, at Christmas or for a birthday, a friendly card is always an appropriate gesture, especially if it has been designed by the sender. With Word 2000 you can create cards with a personal touch by fashioning them to your own taste. There are hardly any limits to what you can do.

Welcome to the Clipart Gallery!

You already know about:

The Word spelling checker   40
Formatting text   50
Saving changes   69
Saving to diskette   72
Moving and copying text   103
The Thesaurus   106
Saving templates   139
Creating a form letter   149
Creating AutoText   179
AutoCorrect   183

You are going to learn about:

Inserting ClipArt pictures   192
Editing pictures   196
The drawing toolbar   202
Casting a shadow   205
WordArt – special text effects   206
Text in pictures   209
Talking pictures   213

Inserting ClipArt pictures

Word offers you several creative options. With the drawing toolbar and a little practice you can produce amazing effects.

However, if you do not possess artistic talent, Word offers you ready-made pictures via the INSERT/PICTURE/CLIPART menu option. These pictures are called **clips**.

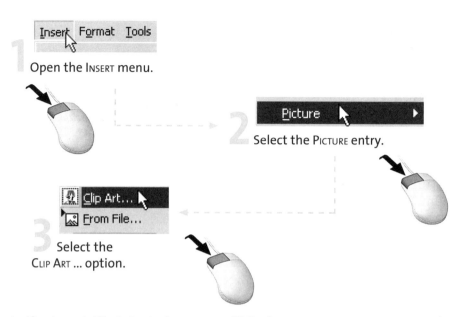

Open the INSERT menu.

Select the PICTURE entry.

Select the
CLIP ART ... option.

In the *Insert ClipArt* window you will find numerous *categories*. With the *All Categories* button you can view all **ClipArt pictures**.

You can select a picture by clicking on it with the mouse. Subsequently, you can also use the cursor keys. Using the scroll bar of the *Insert ClipArt* window,

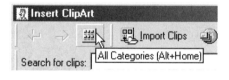

you can browse through all of the pictures, from the first to the last.

Additional ClipArt pictures can be found on the **installation CD-ROM**. You can integrate them with the *Import Clips* button.

You can download free pictures from the **Microsoft Web** page with the *Clips Online* button if you are connected to the **Internet**. There you will also find seasonal clips, thus ensuring that, at Christmas, Santa Claus is available for your Christmas cards!

193

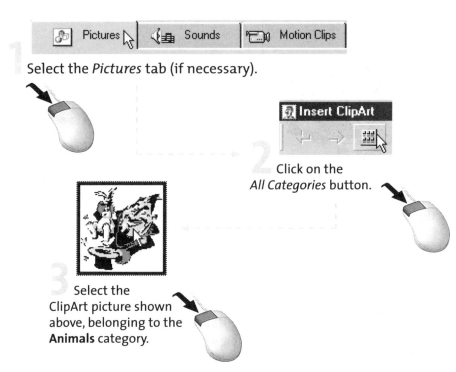

Select the *Pictures* tab (if necessary).

Click on the
All Categories button.

Select the
ClipArt picture shown
above, belonging to the
Animals category.

For the Easter card in this example, choose the magician with the rabbit.

Selecting ClipArt pictures

When you left-click on a picture, a small toolbar opens. With the first button, you insert a ClipArt picture into the document. With the second button, the ClipArt picture can be viewed in a preview window.

Insert
clip

Preview
clip

Select the
Preview clip button.

2 You can see the ClipArt picture in the preview.

3 Close the preview window by clicking on the *Close* button on the title bar.

4 Click on the ClipArt picture again.

5 Insert the ClipArt picture into the document by clicking on the *Insert* button.

6 Close the *Insert* dialog box by clicking on the *Close* button.

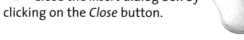

The ClipArt picture has been inserted into the document.

195

Editing pictures

To edit a ClipArt picture it has to be activated. Click on the magician. Small squares – called **sizing handles** – appear.

Click on the picture.

Small squares appear at the edges of the picture.

The frame indicates the size of the ClipArt picture. It disappears by clicking into the document anywhere outside the picture.

Click into the document outside the picture.

The frame of the ClipArt picture has disappeared.

If you position the mouse pointer on one of the sizing handles, you can modify the picture **size** as indicated by the **direction of the arrow**. Holding down the left mouse button you can enlarge or reduce the magician.

Place the mouse pointer on the top right sizing handle.

Modify the size of the ClipArt picture.

If the magician looks slightly too big or too small on your screen, you can simply adjust the **Zoom**. Adjusting the Zoom has no effect on a future print-out (see Chapter 2).

197

To move the picture across the screen, it has to be **formatted**. Place the mouse pointer on the picture and double-click.

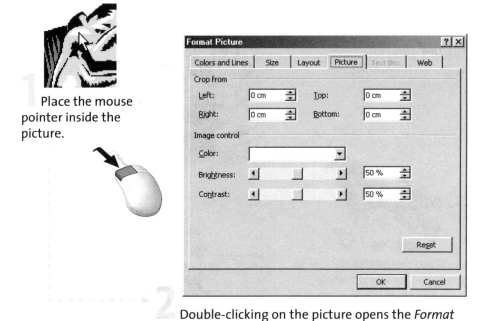

Place the mouse pointer inside the picture.

Double-clicking on the picture opens the *Format Picture* dialog box.

In the *Wrapping style* option of the *Layout* tab in the newly opened dialog box, you can specify how text is later to be placed or flown around the picture.

Overview of wrapping styles

Wrapping style	Effect on text in the document

In line with text

The Magician and the Rabbit. The Magician and the Rabbit. The Magician and the Rabbit. The Magician and the Rabbit.

Square

The Magician and the Rabbit. The Magician and the Rabbit. The Magician and the Rabbit. The Magician and the Rabbit. The Magician and the Rabbit. The Magician

Tight

Wrapping style	Effect on text in the document

Behind text

In front of text

If you want to use a ClipArt picture as a **watermark**, for example in a letter, specify *Behind Text* under *Wrapping style*. Then choose *Watermark* under *Image control/Color* on the *Picture* tab.

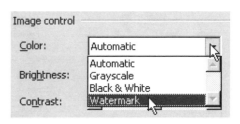

Select the *Layout* tab.

200

2 Select the *Square*
wrapping style.

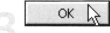

3 Confirm your
entries with the
OK button.

When you move the mouse pointer onto the picture, it
changes to become four arrows. If the pointer takes on this
shape, you can **move** the picture to anywhere inside the
document while keeping the left mouse button pressed.

1 Place the mouse
pointer on the ClipArt
picture.

2 Keeping the left mouse button
pressed, move the ClipArt picture
into the middle of the document.

201

The drawing toolbar

The drawing toolbar has to be opened separately. On the
standard toolbar click on the *Drawing* button. The drawing
toolbar appears, usually at the bottom edge of the screen.

TIP

You can also integrate ClipArt pictures
with the *Insert Clip Art* button on the
drawing toolbar.

Which background would you like?

Now you need the button with the bucket. This allows you
to specify the **fill colour**, that is, the colour an area is to be
painted (filled) with.

1 Activate the
drawing toolbar.

2 Click on the
arrow next to the
Fill Color button.

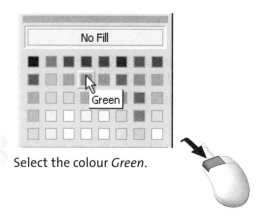

Select the colour *Green*.

If you do not want a fill colour or if you want to delete a previously applied colour click on *No Fill*.

In good shape

With help of the drawing toolbar you can design **shapes** such as rectangles or circles. Is there anything more suitable for Easter than an egg? The most appropriate shape in this case is an **oval**. Click on the button and, keeping the left mouse button pressed, choose the size of the shape.

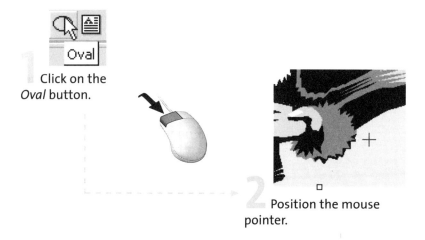

Click on the *Oval* button.

Position the mouse pointer.

203

3 Drag the mouse to open up the shape.

Easter eggs are coloured. It is not a problem to colour these eggs. Again use the *Fill Color* button.

1 Click on the small arrow next to the *Fill Color* button.

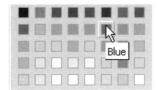

Blue

2 Select a colour.

3 Paint the remaining eggs as in steps 1 and 2.

Casting a shadow

On the drawing toolbar you will find the *Shadow* button. This allows you to add a **shadow** to the picture.

You do not need to apply it to the eggs right now; you can also execute the command for any other picture.

It is possible to cast a shadow from the top, the bottom, the left, or the right. You have several options for applying visual shadow effects.

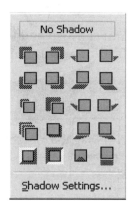

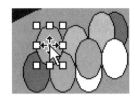

1 Click on an oval or, if you like, an 'egg'.

2 Activate the *Shadow* button.

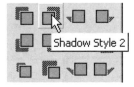

3 Select one of the shadow styles.

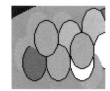

4 Repeat these steps until you are happy with the effect.

WordArt – special text effects

You can also add text, such as the message ' Happy Easter', or, on a birthday card, 'Happy birthday' or 'Many happy returns'.

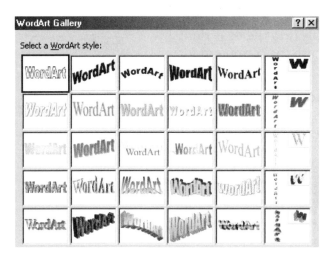

With **WordArt** you can design text individually. Insert a WordArt drawing by clicking on the *Insert WordArt* button on the drawing toolbar. This opens the 'WordArt Gallery' from which you can choose the style you wish.

On the drawing toolbar click on the *Insert WordArt* button.

Double-click on the desired text style.

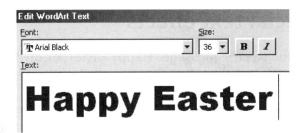

Type 'Happy Easter'.

The *WordArt* toolbar only appears when a WordArt picture is activated.

Confirm your entries with the *OK* button.

The Easter greetings have been integrated into the document. At the same time the *WordArt* toolbar appears on your screen. Whenever a

WordArt picture is activated, the toolbar becomes visible. A

click outside the picture makes the toolbar disappear again.

Click on the *WordArt Shape* button.

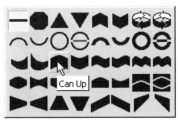

Select a shape.

3 The shape of the lettering has changed.

Moving pictures

You edit WordArt just like a normal picture. When you click on it, the small squares used for changing the size (the sizing handles) appear.

As soon as you position the mouse pointer somewhere inside the text effect, the pointer turns into a 'viewfinder'. Now you can **move** the lettering within the document.

1 Position the mouse pointer on the lettering.

2 Move the WordArt picture slightly upwards.

Underneath the lettering you can see a small yellow **diamond**. When you move the mouse pointer onto the diamond, it again changes its shape. You can use it to modify the lettering.

Head over heels

In Word you have the option to **rotate** pictures up to 360 degrees.

The corresponding button can be found on the **drawing toolbar**.

Click on the button, and the square sizing handles of the WordArt picture turn into small green circles.

As soon as you position the mouse pointer on one of the circles it turns into a **circular arrow**.

Keeping the mouse button pressed, rotate the lettering to the right or to the left, as you wish.

Text in pictures

You can insert text into the magician picture.
To do so you need to insert a **text box** into the picture.

1 Click on the *Text Box* button.

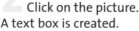

2 Click on the picture. A text box is created.

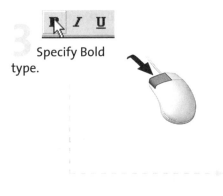

3 Specify Bold type.

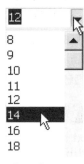

4 Select font size '14'.

5 Type the text 'Mum and dad' into the text box.

Change the size of the text box with the above-mentioned sizing handles. Move the sizing handle until the text 'Mum and dad' fits into a single line.

1 Place the mouse pointer on the right middle sizing handle.

Stretch the text box until the text 'Mum and Dad' fits into a single line.

Place the mouse pointer on the bottom middle sizing handle.

Move the mouse upwards to reduce the height of the text box.

Under *Line Color*, select *No Line* to remove the frame.

However, always remember: to edit a text box it has to be activated. You can see that a text box is activated by the small squares which surround it.

1 Click on the small arrow next to the *Line Color* button.

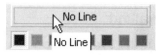

2 Select the *No Line* entry.

The white background of the text box may be irritating. Under **fill colour**, specify *No Fill*. The text box becomes transparent.

1 Click on the arrow next to the *Fill Color* button.

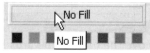

2 Specify *No Fill*.

Mum and Dad

3 Move the **text box** to the bottom margin of the picture.

Talking pictures

You can also make your pictures talk. Again, you use a text box, which you then change into a **callout**.

Click on the *Draw* button located at the very left of the toolbar.

Specify the desired shape of the callout via CHANGE AUTOSHAPE/CALLOUTS.

Click on the *Text Box* button.

Create the text box with a mouse click.

Enter the word 'from' into the text box.

If you have read cartoons such as Asterix or Donald Duck, you are probably familiar with the technique of making characters talk by means of speech balloons.

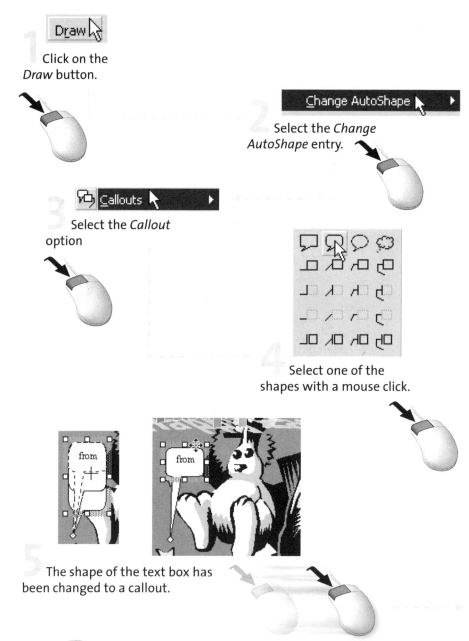

Draw

1 Click on the *Draw* button.

Change AutoShape ▶

2 Select the *Change AutoShape* entry.

Callouts ▶

3 Select the *Callout* option

4 Select one of the shapes with a mouse click.

from *from*

5 The shape of the text box has been changed to a callout.

Change size and position of the callout as you have been shown above.

6 Position the mouse pointer on the small yellow diamond of the callout.

7 Keeping the mouse button pressed, move the pointer until the 'balloon' is placed closer to the mouth.

215

Try to create your own pictures at your leisure with ClipArt pictures and WordArt. You will see how much fun this can be.

What's in this chapter:

Do you scribble down phone numbers, and the birthdays of family members and friends on all sorts of slips of paper? Forget it! With Word, you can create neatly arranged address lists and sort them from A to Z. Never again will you miss important days, events or appointments.

Name○	First·Name○	⊠○	Birthday○	☎○
Summer○	John○	85·York·Road¶ Leeds·LS1·1XY○	03/07/62○	0113-123·456○
Murray○	Sarah○	12·Norfolk·Terrace¶ Newtown·NT1·0ZX○	04/08/78○	0178-327·855○
Duke○	James○	Fairfields¶ Earth·Road¶ Colne·PE17·3NL○	28/11/77○	01487-841·227○
Myers○	Grant○	1·Market·Gardens¶ St·Ives·PE17·3JG○	13/06/65○	01480-363·123○
Myers○	Sarah○	1·Market·Gardens¶ St·Ives·PE17·3JG○	03/01/68○	01480-363·123○
Neugebauer○	James○	3·Yelverton·Road¶ Bournemouth·BH1·0PB○	17○	01703-575·707○
Bennett○	Nick○	17·Cranberry·Avenue¶ Southampton·SO14·0LR○	27/0○	01202-563·795○

You already know about:

Formatting text   50
Saving text   64
Print Preview   75
Printing a document   76
Creating a form letter   149

You are going to learn about:

Inserting tables   220
Table headings   221
Inserting symbols   222
Specifying a table heading   225
Entering text into tables   226
Selecting cells   228
Inserting rows   232
Inserting columns   233
Changing column width   234
Sorting in tables   237
Tables and borders   239
AutoFormat   241
Tables with tabs   242

Inserting tables

You can recognise the importance of tables by the mere fact that there is a separate menu for tables in Word.

To create a table, select the Table/Insert/Table ... menu option, and then specify the **number** of rows and columns you wish. A quicker way to do this is to use the *Insert Table* button.

WHAT'S THIS?

A **table** consists of **rows** and **columns**.

When you click on the button, a submenu opens in which you can determine the **size** – in rows and columns – of the table.

Click on the *Insert Table* button.

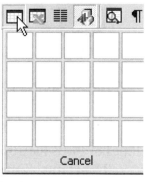

A submenu opens.

WHAT'S THIS?

You do not need to press a mouse button. Simply move the mouse pointer until the desired number of rows and columns is displayed.

Move the mouse pointer.

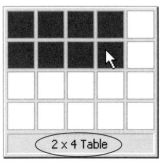

2 Specify two rows and four columns (2 x 4).

3 Confirm with a mouse click.

If you have created an **incorrectly sized table**, you can undo the last command with the *Undo* button on the standard toolbar.

The gridlines of the table appear in the document. For this example, two rows will be enough initially. First set up the columns for name, first name, address and phone number (four columns).

Table headings

In the first row you specify the **table heading**.

The individual fields (boxes) of a table are called **cells**.

Click inside a specific cell and enter the text. In this example the cursor is still flashing in the first cell to the left. Enter 'Name' here. To move to the next cell, press the ⇆ key.

Name¤	
¤	

Click into the first cell and type 'Name'.

Press the
⇥ key.

Name¤	¤
¤	¤

You are now in the second cell.

Alternatively you can move from one cell to another by clicking on it with the mouse. Furthermore, you can move around within tables using the ⬆, ⬇, ⬅ and ➡ keys.

Name¤	First·Name¤
¤	¤

Enter 'First Name'.

First·Name¤	¤ I
¤	¤

Left-click on the next cell.

Inserting symbols

To make the address list visually more appealing, you may insert **symbols**. Select the INSERT/SYMBOL … menu option. Here you will find various symbols and fonts. One of the most interesting of these is **Wingdings**.

Wingdings is a font which contains arrows and symbols.

✎	✂	✄	✍	🖃	📖	▯	☎	🕐	✉	▣	🖬	🖘	🖙
🖫	🖒	🖉	🖎	✚	⚖	🖐	✌	🖝	🖜	◀	▶	✛	☺
✿	☽	☾	♃	❀	♈	♉	♊	♋	♌	♍	♎	♏	♐
◆	✦	•	⌧	⌦	⌘	✾	❀	"	"	▯	◎	◉	◔

Click on the INSERT menu item.

Select the SYMBOL ... option

Activate the *Symbols* tab.

Wingdings	
Symbol	
Tahoma	
Times New Roman	
Webdings	
Wingdings	
Wingdings 2	
Wingdings 3	

Select the *Wingdings* font.

Here you will find symbols for everyday usage. They may appear tiny. However, if you click on one, it is magnified on the screen. Using ⬆, ⬇, ⬅ and ➡ you can move around in the box.

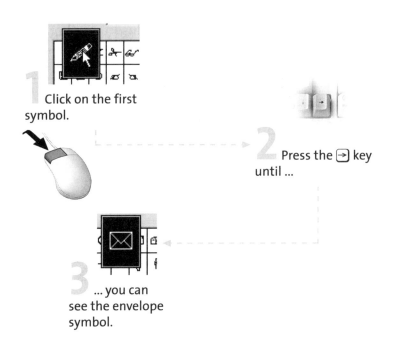

1 Click on the first symbol.

2 Press the → key until ...

3 ... you can see the envelope symbol.

If you want to use a symbol, insert it by double-clicking the left mouse button or by selecting the *Insert* button.

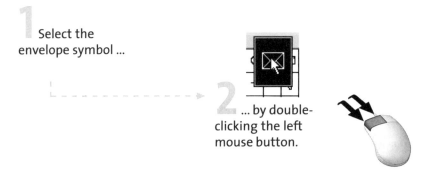

1 Select the envelope symbol ...

2 ... by double-clicking the left mouse button.

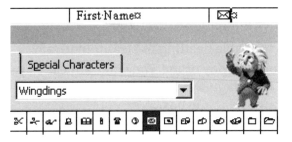

First·Name¤

Special Characters

Wingdings

Above the dialog box you can see the first row of the table, and you will find that Word has inserted the selected symbol.

You can continue working with this dialog box and insert another symbol.

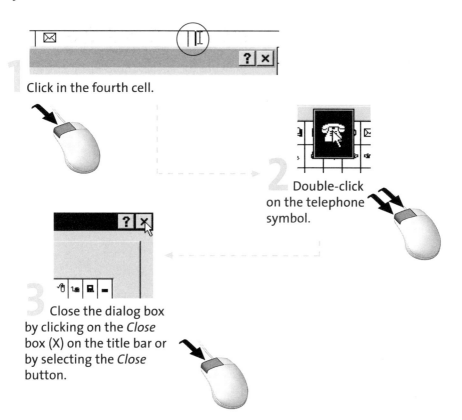

1 Click in the fourth cell.

2 Double-click on the telephone symbol.

3 Close the dialog box by clicking on the *Close* box (X) on the title bar or by selecting the *Close* button.

Specifying a table heading

To make Word recognise the first row of the table as a **heading**, you need to specify this by selecting the TABLE/HEADING ROWS REPEAT menu option. This will be an advantage at a later stage, when you have a lot of entries and the table may be **longer than one page**.

Selecting this option causes the table heading to be automatically inserted on every new page.

225

Open the
TABLE menu and ...

Heading Rows Repeat

... activate the HEADING ROWS REPEAT entry.

The tick mark next to
the entry shows that
a heading is **activated**.

Entering text into tables

After entering the text you move from one cell to the next by
pressing the ⇥ key.

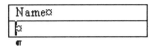

Name¤

¤

Click on the first cell of the
second row.

Name¤
Summer¤

Enter the name 'Summer'.

Name¤	First·Name¤
Summer¤	¤

Press the ⇥ key.

Nameα	First·Nameα
Summerα	Johnɒ

Enter the first name 'John'.

⊠ɒ
ɒ

Press the ⑤ key again.

⊠ɒ
85·York·Roadɒ

Now type in the street '85 York Road'.

⊠ɒ
85·York·Road¶
ɒ

Press the ⏎ key.

⊠ɒ
85·York·Road¶
Leeds·LS1·1XYɒ

Enter the city 'Leeds LS1 1XY'.

☎ɒ
ɒ

Press the ⑤ key.

☎ɒ
0113-123·456ɒ

Enter the phone number '0113- 123 456'.

If you want to create extra addresses you need new rows. When you are in the last cell, press the ⬚ key again. Word automatically inserts a new **table row**.

1 Press the
⬚ key.

Name¤
Summer¤
¤

2 Word inserts a new row. The cursor is flashing in the first cell.

Name¤	First·Name¤	✉¤	☎¤
Summer¤	John¤	85·York·Road¶ Leeds·LS1·1XY¤	0113-123·456¤
Murray¤	Sarah¤	12·Norfolk·Terrace¶ Newtown·NT1·0ZX¤	0178-327·855¤
Duke¤	James¤	Fairfields¶ Earith·Road¶ Colne·PE17·3NL¤	01487-841·227¤
Myers¤	Grant¤	1·Market·Gardens¶ St·Ives·PE17·3JG¤	01480-363·123¤
Neugebauer¤	James¤	3·Yelverton·Road¶ Bournemouth·BH1· 0PB¤	01703-575·707¤
Bennett¤	Nick¤	17·Cranberry·Avenue¶ Southampton·SO14· 0LR¤	01202-563·795¤

3 Enter the following data in the same way:

'Murray ⬚ Sarah ⬚ 12 Norfolk Terrace ↵ Newtown NT1 0ZX ⬚ 0178-327855 ⬚,' and so on.

Selecting cells

To embolden 'Name' and ' First Name' in the table heading, **select** the two cells. Click on the first cell and, keeping the mouse button pressed, **drag** the pointer to the next cell.

1 | Na|me¤ |

Click on the first cell and keep
the mouse button pressed.

2 | Name¤ | First·Name¤ |

Drag the pointer up to the second cell.

3 𝕝 *I* <u>U</u>

Activate bold
formatting.

Selecting columns

You want to centre the contents of the third and fourth column in
the table. First select both. To do this, position the mouse pointer on
the **top row**.

1 Place the
mouse pointer ...

| ✉¤ |
| 85·York·Road¶ |
| Leeds·LS1·1XY¤ |

2 ... on the top row of the third column.

The mouse pointer turns into a black, down-pointing **arrow**. This
means that you can now **select** the whole column by left-clicking it.

To include the next column, drag the **selection** across. Now click on the *Center* button. The contents have been centred.

Select the third column with a mouse click.

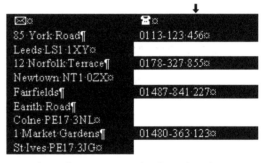

Drag the selection into the fourth column.

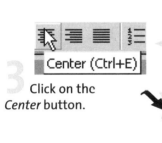

Center (Ctrl+E)

Click on the *Center* button.

Selecting rows

Slightly enlarge the table heading by selecting a different type size. First you need to select the row.

When you position the mouse pointer in front of a row, it changes its **pointing direction**.

Left-click and the row is **selected**. If you want to include several rows, simply drag the selection up or down.

Name¤	First-Name¤
Summer¤	John¤

Position the mouse pointer in front of the row.

Name¤	First-Name¤	✉¤	☎¤
Summer¤	John¤	85·York·Road¶ Leeds·LS1·1XY¤	0113-123-4:

Left-click.

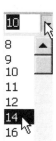

Enlarge the type size to '14'.

231

Inserting rows

In this example you meet Mr 'Myers, Grant'. He has just got married. You would like to insert his wife into your address list, too.

Grant¤	Myers¤	1·Market·Gardens¶ St·Ives·PE17·3JG¤	01480-363·123¤
Neugebauer¤	James¤	3·Yelverton·Road¶ Bournemouth·BH1· 0PB¤	01703-575·707¤

1 Select the row.

2 Click on the INSERT ROWS button.

Myers¤	Sarah¤	1·Market·Gardens¶ St·Ives·PE17·3JG¤	01480-363·123¤

3 Fill in the remaining information.

Table   Window   Help

✏ Draw Table

Insert

Delete

Inserting columns

As soon as you **select** a column the *Insert Rows* button changes into *Insert Columns*.

You want to insert a column called 'Birthdays' into the table, so that you always remember to send a card.

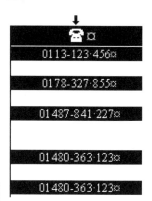

1 Select the column.

Birthday○
03/07/62○
04/08/78○
28/11/77○
13/06/65○
03/01/68○
17/07/78○
27/07/78○

3 Enter the birthdays.

2 Click on the *Insert Columns* button.

233

Changing column width

If, after you have inserted the additional column, you can no longer view the table very clearly, you could adjust the zoom, so that the table fits again onto the screen. However, the lettering would then be so small that you would need a magnifying glass in front of your screen to be able to figure it out.

CAUTION

With the TABLE/AUTOFIT menu option the size of columns and rows can be adjusted automatically.

Columns such as 'Name' or 'First Name' take up unnecessary space, but you can reduce them.

Name○	First·Name○
Summer○	┥┝John○

1 Place the mouse pointer on the line between the 'First Name' and 'Name' columns.

2 The mouse pointer changes its appearance.

CAUTION

If while dragging you keep **the right mouse button pressed as well**, you can see the exact column width on the **ruler**.

Keeping the left mouse button pressed, drag the line. A ruler is displayed above.

Of course you do not need to adopt the measurements of this example, so long as you understand it in principle.

TIP

In particularly large tables you can choose **landscape format** on the *Paper Size* tab in the FILE/PAGE SETUP menu option.

Orientation

[A] C Portrait
    ⊙ Landscape

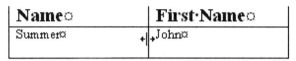

Position the mouse pointer exactly on the column separation line.

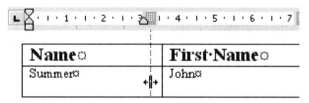

Keeping the mouse button pressed, push the mouse pointer a little to the right ...

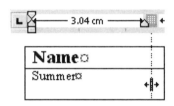

... and press the right mouse button at the same time.

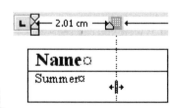

Set the new column width.

235

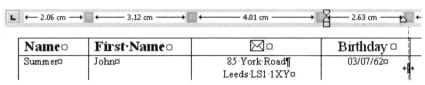

Name¤	First·Name¤	⌧¤	Birthday ¤
Summer¤	John¤	85·York·Road¶ Leeds·LS1·1XY¤	03/07/62¤

5 Adjust the column width for 'First Name, Address, Birthday'.

6 To be able to see the last column 'Phone Number' completely, move the bottom scroll bar to the right (if necessary).

☏ ¤	¤
01480-363·123¤	¤
01487-841·227¤	¤

7 Move the last column line.

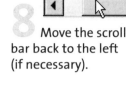

8 Move the scroll bar back to the left (if necessary).

With the *Column* tab the TABLE/TABLE PROPERTIES menu option you can specify the width of columns with precise measurements.

You use the buttons shown below to move from one column to the next. To be able to perform this operation, the insertion point needs to be inside the table.

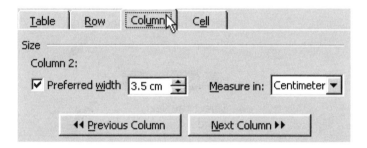

Sorting in tables

Your address list is almost finished. However, the individual names are still in a haphazard order. Sort the names from **A to Z**.

However, this example poses a small problem. There are persons who share the **same name**: Grant and Sarah Myers.

For **sorting**, the insertion point needs to be **inside the table**.

The address list entries should be sorted as in a phone directory, that is first by **surname**, then by **first name**.

237

Name¤	First·Name¤	✉¤	Birthday¤	☎¤
Summer¤	John¤	85·York·Road¶ Leeds·LS1·1XY¤	03/07/62¤	0113-123·456¤
Murray¤	Sarah¤	12·Norfolk·Terrace¶ Newtown·NT1·0ZX¤	04/08/78¤	0178-327·855¤
Duke¤	James¤	Fairfields¶ Earith·Road¶ Colne·PE17·3NL¤	28/11/77¤	01487-841·227¤
Myers¤	Grant¤	1·Market·Gardens¶ St·Ives·PE17·3JG¤	13/06/65¤	01480-363·123¤
Myers¤	Sarah¤	1·Market·Gardens¶ St·Ives·PE17·3JG¤	03/01/68¤	01480-363·123¤
Neugebauer¤	James¤	3·Yelverton·Road¶ Bournemouth·BH1·0PB¤	17/07/78¤	01703-575·707¤
Bennett¤	Nick¤	17·Cranberry·Avenue¶ Southampton·SO14·0LR¤	27/07/78¤	01202-563·795¤

Open the TABLE menu.

Select the SORT command.

As soon as you activate the menu option, Word automatically selects the table in the background.

You specify the sorting criteria. The first criterion is the surname; the second one is the first name.

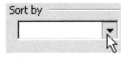

Click on the arrow under *sort by*.

Select 'First Name'.

Confirm with the *OK* button.

Name¤	First·Name¤	✉¤	Birthday ¤	☎¤
Myers¤	Grant¤	1·Market·Gardens¶ St·Ives·PE17·3JG¤	13/06/65¤	01480-363·123¤
Duke¤	James¤	Fairfields¶ Earith·Road¶ Colne·PE17·3NL¤	28/11/77¤	01487-841·227¤
Neugebauer¤	James¤	3·Yelverton·Road¶ Bournemouth·BH1·0PB¤	17/07/78¤	01703-575·707¤
Summer¤	John¤	85·York·Road¶ Leeds·LS1·1XY¤	03/07/62¤	0113-123·456¤
Bennett¤	Nick¤	17·Cranberry·Avenue¶ Southampton·SO14·0LR¤	27/07/78¤	01202-563·795¤
Murray¤	Sarah¤	12·Norfolk·Terrace¶ Newtown·NT1·0ZX¤	04/08/78¤	0178-327·855¤
Myers¤	Sarah¤	1·Market·Gardens¶ St·Ives·PE17·3JG¤	03/01/68¤	01480-363·123¤

You deselect the table with a mouse click anywhere in the table or the document.

Tables and borders

You can use the table pencil to design your own tables, either by selecting the TABLE/DRAW TABLE menu option or by clicking on the *Tables and Borders* button on the standard toolbar.

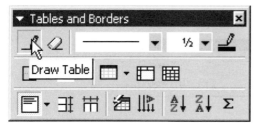

No matter which way you choose: an additional **toolbar** is opened on the screen. It offers you a multitude of opportunities. You already know the function of the buttons *A to Z* and *Z to A*.

They are used for sorting in tables, but only by the first column. Furthermore, you can also find the **table pencil** in this toolbar.

When you click on the *Draw Table* button, the mouse pointer changes into a pencil. You return to the 'normal' mouse pointer by clicking on the button a second time or by pressing the (Esc) key.

With the pencil as mouse pointer you can design tables and set the

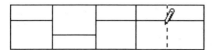

type and size of the individual cells according to your requirements, as you can see in the slightly 'abstract' example on the left.

Deleting table lines

The button with the **eraser** has probably already caught your attention. You can actually use it for erasing. All you need to do is click on the button, and the mouse pointer changes its shape.

Then, in a table, simply click on the **line** which you want to **remove**. You cancel the function by clicking once more on the **eraser** button or by pressing the (Esc) key.

Inserting border lines

Cells in tables can be highlighted with a border – 'be framed', so to speak. The black lines show you

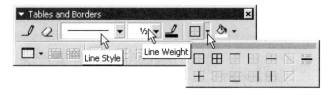

where the border will be: left, right, top, bottom. You can also specify line type and weight.

AutoFormat

With the TABLE/TABLE AUTOFORMAT menu option you can specify a particular look for a table.

Name¤	First·Name¤	⊠¤	Birthday ¤	☎¤
Summer¤	John¤	85·York·Road¶ Leeds·LS1·1XY¤	03/07/62¤	0113-123·456¤
Murray¤	Sarah¤	12·Norfolk·Terrace¶ Newtown·NT1·0ZX¤	04/08/78¤	0178-327·855¤
Duke¤	James¤	Fairfields¶ Earith·Road¶ Colne·PE17·3NL¤	28/11/77¤	01487-841·227¤
Myers¤	Grant¤	1·Market·Gardens¶ St·Ives·PE17·3JG¤	13/06/65¤	01480-363·123¤
Myers¤	Sarah¤	1·Market·Gardens¶ St·Ives·PE17·3JG¤	03/01/68¤	01480-363·123¤
Neugebauer¤	James¤	3·Yelverton·Road¶ Bournemouth·BH1·0PB¤	17/07/78¤	01703-575·707¤
Bennett¤	Nick¤	17·Cranberry·Avenue¶ Southampton·SO14·0LR¤	27/07/78¤	01202-563·795¤

Place the insertion point inside the table.

In the TABLE menu, select ...

... the TABLE AUTOFORMAT entry.

Here you have a choice of several pre-set tables. In the preview you can get an idea of how they will look.

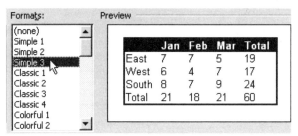

Select a format.

Confirm your entries with the *OK* button.

Tables with tabs

When you press the ⊡ key, the cursor **jumps** forward in the document. This is not only quicker, but it also saves you pressing the space bar umpteen times. In connection with tabs several terms such as tabulator, tab stop or tabulator stop are used which all mean the same thing.

The easiest and quickest way to set tabs is with the **ruler**.

You can show the ruler on your screen in two ways.

Place the mouse pointer **exactly below** the formatting toolbar.

After a few moments, the ruler appears.

Move the mouse pointer back into the document. The ruler disappears from the screen.

The disadvantage of this method is that the ruler is not permanently displayed. You can also show the ruler in the following way.

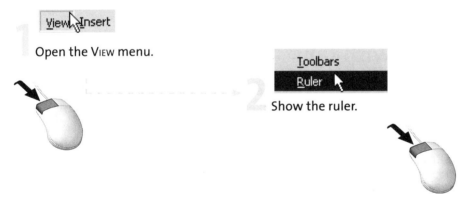

Open the VIEW menu.

Show the ruler.

Now the ruler is permanently visible on your screen. You can hide the ruler again using the same procedure.

Setting tabs

To the left in front of the ruler you will see an 'L'. This means that you are currently setting **left aligned** tabs when you click the mouse in the ruler. As usual, the text is aligned from left to right.

243

Move the mouse pointer into the ruler and click the mouse button. The tab stop appears.

1 Open a new document for this exercise.

Left Tab

2 Set the first tab.

When you press the ⇥ key, the cursor 'jumps' forward to a point exactly **under the tab**.

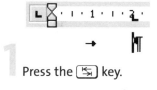

1 Press the ⇥ key.

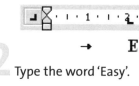

2 Type the word 'Easy'.

When you click again on the symbol in front of the ruler, the tab changes.

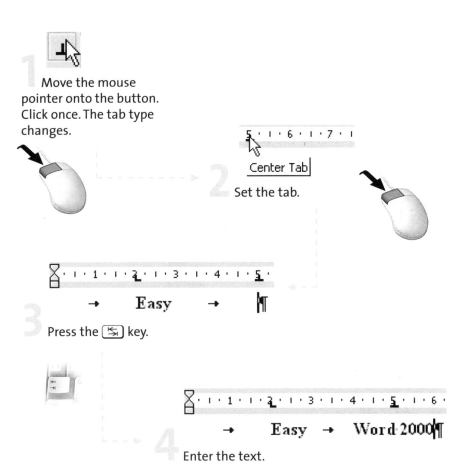

1 Move the mouse pointer onto the button. Click once. The tab type changes.

2 Set the tab.

3 Press the key.

4 Enter the text.

In a **centered** tab the text aligns at its middle.

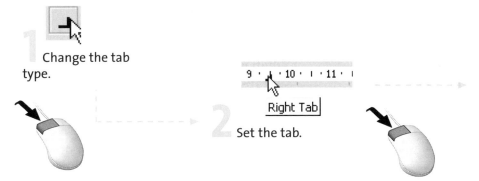

1 Change the tab type.

2 Set the tab.

245

I · 9 · ↓ · 10

3 Type '£'.

In a **right aligned** tab stop the text aligns right to left.

1 Change the tab type.

·12· I ·13· I ·:

2 Set the tab.

I ·12· I ·1

29,95¶

3 Press the ⇆ key. Type the number '29.95'.

The **decimal** tab stop is often used for **numbers**. The decimal points of the individual values are then arranged exactly beneath one another.

When you then press the ↵ key, the set tabs are taken over into the next line.

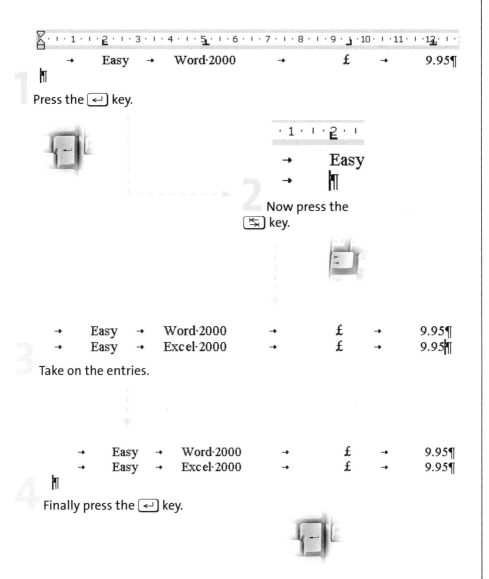

1 Press the ⏎ key.

2 Now press the ⇆ key.

3 Take on the entries.

4 Finally press the ⏎ key.

Shifting tabs

Have you written one or more lines making use of tabs? For **one line** you only need to move the tabs **keeping the mouse button pressed**. If **several lines** are affected, you need to **select** them first.

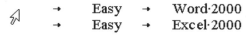

Position the mouse pointer.

Click with the mouse.
The first line has been selected.

Select both lines.

Click on the tab symbol, and keep
the mouse button pressed.

Still keeping the mouse button
pressed, move the tab ...

.... to a new position
on the ruler.

Removing tabs

Removing tabs is as easy as can be. Click on a tab symbol directly on the ruler, hold down the mouse button and drag it into the white area, that is, into the writing area of Word.

→   Easy
→   Easy

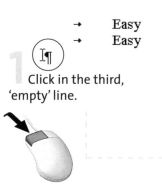

1 Click in the third, 'empty' line.

I · 2 · I · 3 · I

Left Tab

→ Easy

2 Click on the tab symbol, keeping the left mouse button pressed.

· L · 3 · I · 4

Left Tab

3 Drag downwards.

· I · 2 · I · 3 · I · 4

     Easy   →
     Easy   →

4 As soon as you release the mouse button, the tab disappears.

When you **double-click on a tab** in the ruler, the *Tabs* dialog box appears, in which you can, besides other things, remove all tabs with the *Clear All* button.

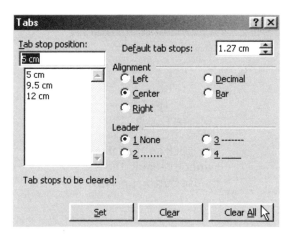

Practise, practise ... and practise again!

In this exercise you practise **sorting** in tables. This time you will not list text but **numbers**.

Use the *New* button to create a **new** document.

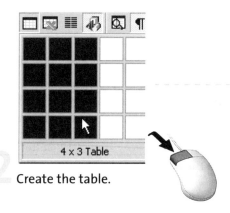

Create the table.

Name¤	First·Name¤	Score¤
¤	¤	¤

Enter the column headings ('Name', 'First Name', 'Score').

Select the whole row.

Make the cell
contents bold.

Heading Rows Repeat

In the T<small>ABLE</small> menu select the H<small>EADING</small> R<small>OWS</small>
R<small>EPEAT</small> entry.

Name¤	First Name¤	Score¤
Miller¤	Paul¤	54¤
Lucy¤	Dugdale¤	99¤
Louise¤	Pomfret¤	85¤

Type the data into the appropriate rows.

8 Open the TABLE menu.

9 Select the SORT entry.

10 The person with the **highest score** is to be listed at the top. Specify 'Score' under *Sort by*.

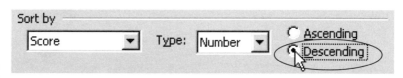

11 As you do not want to sort the scores from 0 to 100, but from **100 to 0**, activate the *Descending* option.

Confirm your entries with the *OK* button.

Name	First Name	Score
Lucy	Dugdale	99
Louise	Pomfret	85
Miller	Paul	54

12 The result of the sorting process: the winner with the highest score is shown at the top.

13

What's in this chapter:

You do not have to accept Word's user interface as it is. If you use functions again and again but which are not on any of the toolbars, just 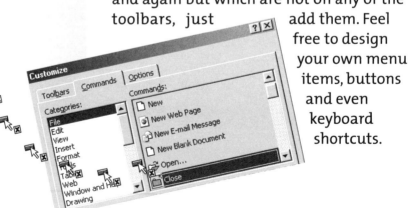 add them. Feel free to design your own menu items, buttons and even keyboard shortcuts.

You already know about:

Saving changes	69
Moving and copying text	103
The Thesaurus	106
Saving templates	139
Creating a form letter	149
Creating AutoText	179
AutoCorrect	183
Inserting ClipArt images	192
Inserting tables	220
Inserting symbols	222

You are going to learn about:

Integrating buttons	256
Creating menu options	266
Defining your own keyboard shortcuts	270

Integrating buttons

In Word you can create your own **buttons**. At the right-hand border of the Word window, on the formatting toolbar, you can see the button called *More Buttons*.

When you click on it, the *Add or Remove Buttons* command opens.

1 On the formatting toolbar, click on the *More Buttons* button .

Add or Remove Buttons ▾

2 Move the mouse pointer onto the *Add or Remove Buttons* command.

With these entries you can add further buttons to the formatting toolbar.

A tick mark in front of an entry indicates that the button is already on the formatting toolbar.

✓	**Style:**	
✓	**Font:**	
✓	**Font Size:**	
✓ **B**	**Bold**	Ctrl+B
✓ *I*	**Italic**	Ctrl+I
✓ <u>U</u>	**Underline**	Ctrl+U
✓	**Align Left**	Ctrl+L
✓	**Center**	Ctrl+E
✓	**Align Right**	Ctrl+R
✓	**Justify**	Ctrl+J
✓	**Numbering**	
✓	**Bullets**	
✓	**Decrease Indent**	
✓	**Increase Indent**	
✓	**Borders**	
✓	**Highlight**	
✓ **A**	**Font Color**	

═ 1.5 Spacing   Ctrl+5

The *1.5 Spacing* button sets the line spacing in paragraphs to one and a half lines. In this example you will integrate this button into the formatting toolbar.

Click on the *1.5 Spacing* entry.

Click anywhere in the document.

The button is now included on the **Formatting toolbar**.

You can remove it using the same method.

Click on the button *More Buttons*.

Add or Remove Buttons ▾

Move the mouse pointer on the *Add or Remove Buttons* command.

Select the *1.5 Spacing* entry.

257

The *1.5 Spacing* button has been removed from the formatting toolbar.

You can also add buttons to the **Standard toolbar**.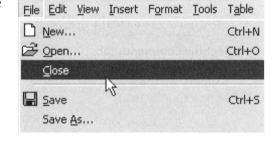

At the right end of the standard toolbar you will notice a button with a downward pointing arrow. When you click on it you can, as described for the formatting toolbar above, add and remove buttons on the standard toolbar.

Another example:

In the FILE menu, you can see the CLOSE command. This is used to close a document without exiting Word. However, you always need to open the menu and click on the menu entry.

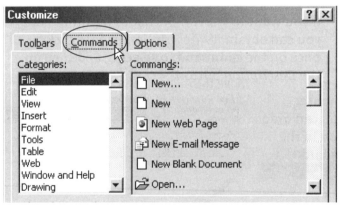

You could close documents more quickly with a button.

However, there is the *Close* function, which you can add as a button to the standard toolbar.

Of course you can also integrate other buttons. All the functions are listed on the *Commands* tab under the TOOLS/CUSTOMIZE menu option.

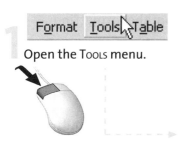

Open the Tools menu.

Click on the Customize command.

Select the *Commands* tab.

On the left side of the dialog box you can see several categories.

The *Close* function can be found in the *File* category.

If you want to know more about a command, you can obtain its **description** by first clicking once on the command to select it, and then on the *Description* button.

Keeping the left mouse button pressed, you can **drag** the required button to the others on the standard toolbar.

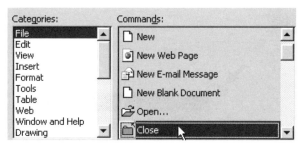

From the *Categories* box, select the *File* entry (if needed). Click on the *Close* command.

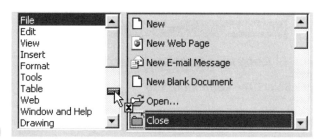

Keeping the left mouse button pressed, ...

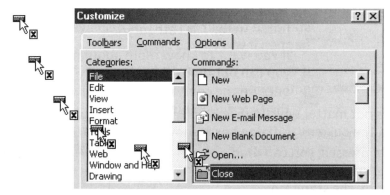

... drag the *Close* command onto the **Standard toolbar**.

4 Position the button.

5 The *Close* button is in its new place.

6 Close the dialog box with the appropriate button.

When you move the mouse pointer onto the new button on the standard toolbar, ScreenTips displays what would happen if you clicked on it.

If you wish to **remove a button** select the TOOLS/CUSTOMIZE menu option.

It does not matter which **tab** is visible in the foreground. What counts is that the *Customize* **dialog box** is shown on your screen.

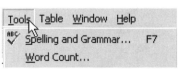

1 Open the TOOLS menu.

261

Select the CUSTOMIZE command.

Keeping the mouse button pressed, **drag** the *Close* button from the Standard toolbar into the *Customize* dialog box.

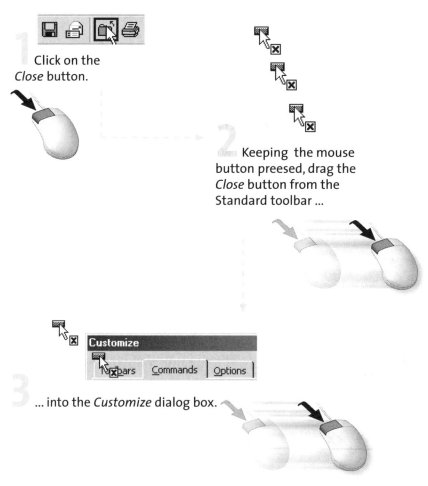

Click on the *Close* button.

Keeping the mouse button preesed, drag the *Close* button from the Standard toolbar ...

... into the *Customize* dialog box.

The *Close* button has disappeared from the Standard toolbar.

Editing button images

You can redesign the look of a button, including the **button image**, via the TOOLS/CUSTOMIZE menu option. The *Customize* dialog box needs to be active on your screen.

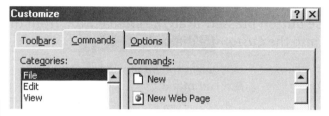

Important: can you see the *Customize* dialog box on your screen? If not select the TOOLS/CUSTOMIZE menu option.

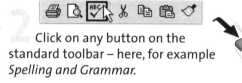

Click on any button on the standard toolbar – here, for example *Spelling and Grammar*.

Clicking the **right mouse button** opens a context menu. Here you can change **the look of button images**.

Next to the name of the activated button you notice a number of commands.

Using the *Delete* command is an alternative way of **removing a button** from the toolbar.

263

✓ Defa_u_lt Style
 _T_ext Only (Always)
 Text _O_nly (in Menus)

1 Open the context menu by
clicking the right mouse button.

✓ Defa_u_lt Style
 _T_ext Only (Always)
 Text _O_nly (in Menus)
 Image _a_nd Text

2 Select the *Image and
Text* command.

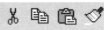
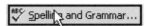

3   Spelling and Grammar...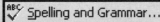

The descriptive text has been added to the image.

 Spelli_n_g and Grammar...

4 Move the mouse pointer onto
the button image, and right-click on it.

Defa_u_lt Style
 _T_ext Only (Always)
 Text _O_nly (in Menus)
✓ Image _a_nd Text

5 When you select the
Default Style command ...

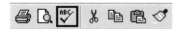

6 ... the button image reverts to its original appearance.

7 Place the mouse pointer on the button image again and right-click on it.

Copy Button Image
Paste Button Image
Reset Button Image
Edit Button Image...
Change Button Image ▶

8 Select the *Change Button Image* command.

9 Click on any button image.

10 The newly selected button image appears on the Standard toolbar.

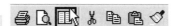

11 Again, right-click on the button image.

265

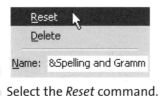

Select the *Reset* command.

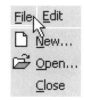

The button image reverts to its original appearance.

As soon as you leave the *Customize* dialog box, the black border around the button disappears.

Creating menu options

Similarly to adding a new button to the Standard toolbar you can also add menu options. Take, for example, the C\ose A\l command, and add it to the F\le menu.

File Edit
New...
Open...
Close

Close and Close All?

What is the difference? With the C\ose command you can only close one document at a time, while the C\ose A\l command closes all open documents at once.

Menu option	Effect
F\le/C\ose	Closes **one document** on the screen at a time. The command needs to be called up each time.
F\le/C\ose A\l	Closes **all documents** on the screen. The command needs to be called up only once.

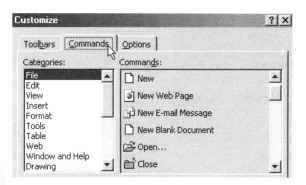

Use the Tools/Customize menu option to activate the
Commands tab (if necessary).

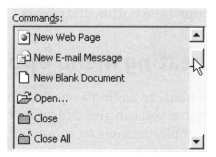

Use the scroll bar in the dialog
box to select ...

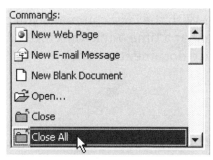

... the Close All command.

267

Open the menu – here, for example, the FILE menu. This is where the CLOSE ALL command will be inserted.

Starting in the *Customize* dialog box, drag the command ...

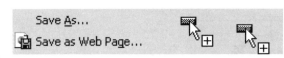

... into the open FILE menu.

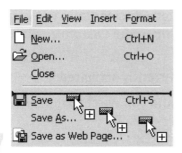

7 Establish the position of the command within the open FILE menu. The black line indicates where the new command will appear, as soon as you release the mouse button.

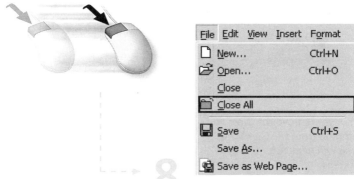

8 The new CLOSE ALL command is now available in the FILE menu.

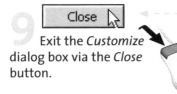

9 Exit the *Customize* dialog box via the *Close* button.

Open the FILE menu. You will see that the new command has been inserted.

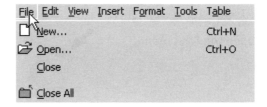

269

Should you want to remove a menu option – incidentally, you can remove any menu option – you need to open the *Customize* **dialog box** via the Tools/Customize menu option.

It does not matter which of the tabs is currently activated.

Open the File menu and **drag** the command you want to remove into the *Customize* **dialog box**.

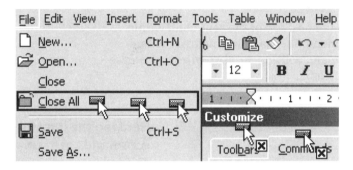

Do not yet remove the Close All command from the File menu, as you will need it for the next few steps.

Defining your own keyboard shortcuts

You can also define new keyboard shortcuts.

Again we take the Close All command as an example.

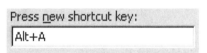

Open the Tools menu.

Select the CUSTOMIZE command.

Click on the *Keyboard* button.

Here too the individual commands are sub-divided into categories. In this example you need the category *File*.

As it happens, the command you are looking for is located at the very top.

Word will advise you whether a **keyboard shortcut** is already **taken** by a different command.

For the FILE/CLOSE ALL command you could, for example, select the Alt+A keyboard shortcut.

Keyboard shortcut	Word reports ...
Press new shortcut key: Alt+A	Currently assigned to: [unassigned]
Press new shortcut key: Ctrl+O	Currently assigned to: FileOpen

Now press the 〔Alt〕+〔A〕 key combination. As soon as you release the keys, they appear in the *Current keys* box. Then click on the *Assign* button.

This means that the selected keyboard shortcut is assigned to the FILE/CLOSE ALL command.

Current keys:

Alt+A

Press <u>n</u>ew shortcut key:

1 Click on the *Press new shortcut key* box.

2 Keep the 〔Alt〕 key pressed.

3 Press the 〔A〕 key.

Press <u>n</u>ew shortcut key:

Alt+A

4 Release the keys. The keyboard shortcut appears in the box.

Assign...
<u>R</u>emove
Re<u>s</u>et All...

5 Confirm with the *Assign* button.

The associated shortcut keys appear in the box under *Current keys*.

Until you change the selected keys, they will be associated with the *Close All* command.

To **remove** a shortcut key, click on the associated command and on the current keyboard shortcut. Then confirm the operation with the *Remove* button.

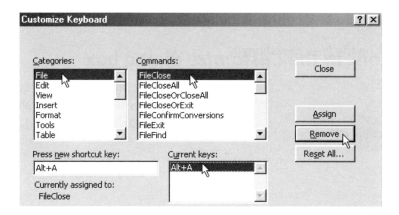

Now you need to close the two dialog boxes which are currently open on the screen.

First close one dialog box ...

... and then the other.

273

Now you can go and try out your new keyboard shortcut. However, it is also possible to check without so much effort whether everything is defined correctly.

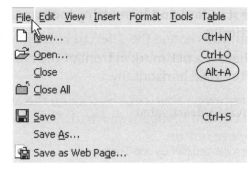

Open the FILE menu. To the right of the CLOSE ALL command you will notice the keyboard shortcut ($\boxed{\text{Alt}}$+$\boxed{\text{A}}$) that you have created.

Options in the *Customize* dialog box

Clicking on an **option** changes the **settings** of Word.

On the *Options* tab in the *Customize* dialog box you will find a few useful entries which change the look of your screen in Word.

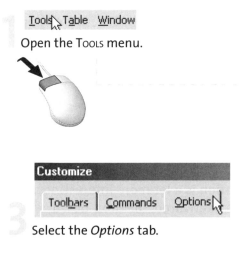

Open the TOOLS menu.

Click on the CUSTOMIZE command.

Select the *Options* tab.

The **standard and formatting toolbars** are tiled either **horizontally** or **vertically**.

If there is a tick mark in front of the entry, click on it. Now the toolbars will be tiled horizontally.

Activated/deactivated	Explanation
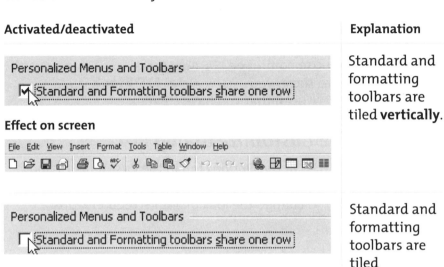	Standard and formatting toolbars are tiled **vertically**.
	Standard and formatting toolbars are tiled **horizontally**.

By clicking on the *Large icons* option you can select a (much) larger display of the toolbars.

Other
☐ Large icons

You can see the bigger buttons in the background of the *Customize* dialog box without having to leave it.

The *List font names in their font* option is a lot more interesting.

Other
☐ Large icons
☑ List font names in their font

When activated, the drop-down *Font* list will display font previews.

275

Of course after selecting the option you first need to exit the *Customize* dialog box.

When you click on the *Show shortcut keys in ScreenTips* option, the associated **keyboard shortcut** is displayed in **ScreenTips**, as soon as you move the mouse pointer on a button – here *Save*. Again you first need to exit the *Customize* dialog box.

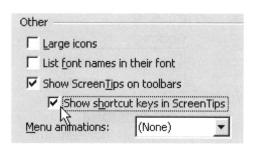

Animations

Word offers you visual effects with the 'menu animation' function. This allows you to determine the way menu items open.

You can see the selected animation by opening any menu item.

If you do not want menu animation, simply specify *(None)* in the list.

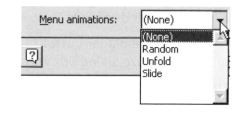

Practise, practise ... and practise again!

So far in this chapter you have had to select the TOOLS/CUSTOMIZE menu option to get into the *Customize* dialog box.

You can shorten this procedure by means of a shortcut key. Use the key combination ⌐Alt⌐+⌐P⌐. This keyboard shortcut is not yet assigned to any other command in Word.

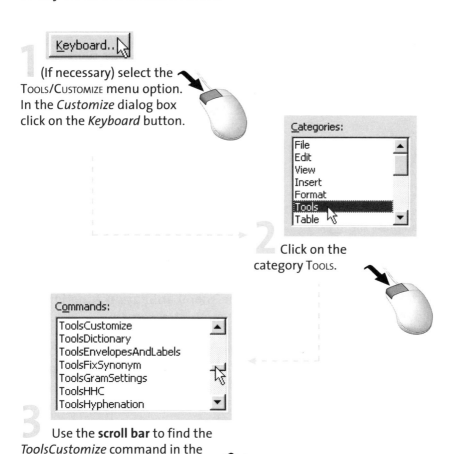

1 (If necessary) select the TOOLS/CUSTOMIZE menu option. In the *Customize* dialog box click on the *Keyboard* button.

2 Click on the category TOOLS.

3 Use the **scroll bar** to find the *ToolsCustomize* command in the dialog box.

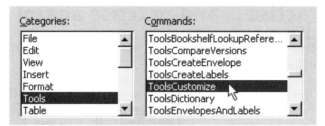

Select the *ToolsCustomize* command.

Press new shortcut key:

Click in the field under *Press new shortcut key*.

Hold down the [Alt] key, then press the [P] key.

Press new shortcut key:

Alt+P|

Currently assigned to:
[unassigned]

As soon as you release both keys, the keyboard shortcut appears in the box.

Assign

Remove

Reset All...

Click on the *Assign* button.

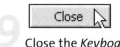

9 Close the *Keyboard* dialog box.

10 Exit the *Customize* dialog box via the *Close* button.

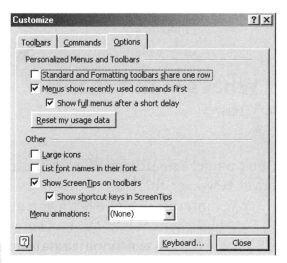

11 When you now press the shortcut keys Alt+P, you immediately get into the *Customize* dialog box.

When you now open the Tools menu, you will see the keyboard shortcut you have just created next to the Customize command.

14

What's in this chapter:

Don't panic! You are not going to write a novel. However, this chapter might be of interest to you, even if you are no Dickens. It is about footnotes; that is, additional remarks on the bottom margin of a page. With 'drop caps' you can graphically design pages, with large dropped initial letters of a paragraph.

If you write more than one page, what do you need? Page numbers, of course. This chapter will discuss all these options.

Footnotes and page numbers

You already know about:

Saving changes 69
Moving and copying text 103
The Thesaurus 106
Saving templates 139
Creating a form letter 149
Creating AutoText 179
AutoCorrect 183
Inserting ClipArt pictures 192
Inserting tables 220
Inserting symbols 222
Integrating buttons 256
Creating menu options 266
Defining your own keyboard shortcuts 270

You are going to learn about:

Inserting footnotes 282
Editing footnotes 286
Inserting page numbers 293

Inserting footnotes

You have probably heard about footnotes before and what they are.

Shakespeare[1] was man who wrote beautiful poetry.

Footnotes are frequently used in books and appear on the **bottom margin** of the page. They provide additional information on the text in the page.

In this example you will write 'Shakespeare'. With the aid of a footnote you will then explain that he was an English poet.

Footnotes	All Footnotes	▼	Close

[1] English poet

Footnotes are frequently used in academic papers or in reports about projects or a company's products to provide additional information.

If this additional information is collected and displayed at the end of a text covering several pages, it is referred to as endnotes.

A crucial factor for what you see when you are creating the footnote is the **view** which you have chosen.

To proceed uniformly throughout the next steps, select

View	Insert	Format
📄 Normal		
🌐 Web Layout		
🖥 Print Layout		

[1] English poet

Normal view. In **Print Layout** view, inputting of the footnote would look like this.

Open the VIEW menu.

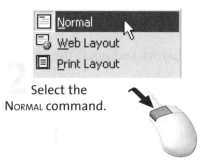

Select the
NORMAL command.

To create footnotes, you first need to enter text.
Then you place the cursor behind the word to which
you want to add a footnote.

Recently I was in Stratford-upon-Avon. There I met a certain William Shakespeare. Later
Alan Shearer joined us.

Enter the above text.

William Shakespeare. Later

Place the cursor **immediately behind** 'Shakespeare'.

Open the INSERT menu.

Select the FOOTNOTE
command.

In the *Footnote and Endnote* dialog box you could change a few more things.

In this example, however, this is not necessary.

Under *Insert* you can specify whether the additions should appear on the current page or, by activating the *Endnote* entry, at the end of the document, for example a several page long manuscript.

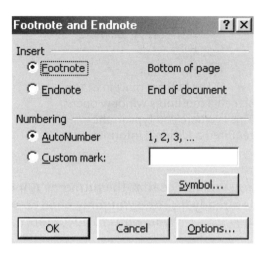

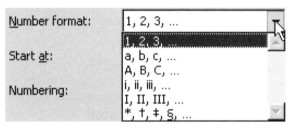

Via the *Options* button you can change the consecutive numbering from Arabic numerals 1, 2, 3, ... into, for example, I, II, III, ... or A, B, C, ...

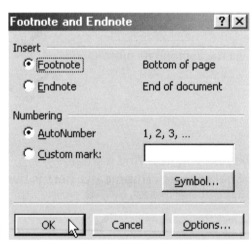

Click on the *OK* button of the *Footnote and Endnote* dialog box.

At the bottom margin of the screen a footnotes window opens. This is where you type in the required additional information.

You will notice that the numeral '1', indicating the first footnote, is already inserted. You only need to enter the text.

Enter the word 'Poet' as the first footnote.

Close the footnote window via the appropriate button.

The window disappears. In the text you now find a small, superscript '1' after the word 'Shakespeare'. This means: **here is the first footnote**.

William Shakespeare^1. Later

Move the mouse pointer onto the number '1'.

285

Shakespeare⌐Later

The contents are displayed ...

Poet

Shakespeareᴵ. Later

... in a yellow box.

Editing footnotes

In this example you want to add more text to the first footnote. So far it consists only of the word 'Poet'. The contents need to be changed to 'English poet'.

To edit an existing footnote, choose the FOOTNOTES option in the VIEW menu.

Adding to footnotes

An even quicker alternative is to **double-click** on the superscript '1' after 'Shakespeare'. This takes you straight to the footnote window.

William Shakespeare⌐Later

Place the mouse pointer on footnote '1'.

Double-click on the footnote.

Footnotes	All Footnotes

    ‖ Poet

The footnote window opens at the bottom of the screen.

Press the ➜ key
twice.

Footnotes | All Footnotes

¹ |Poet

The insertion point is flashing
in front of the word 'Poet'.

Footnotes | All Footnotes

¹ English p|oet

Type the word 'English', press the
⊏___⊐ bar once, then change the upper
case 'P' of 'Poet' into a lower case 'p'.

Footnotes | All Footnotes   ▼ Clo

¹ English p|oet

Close the window with the *Close* button.

William Shakespeare⌐Later

Move the mouse pointer onto the footnote in the text.

English poet

William Shakespeare¹. Later
The new contents are displayed.

Inserting further footnotes

Recently I was in Stratford-upon-Avon. There I met a certain William Shakespeare[1]. Later Alan Shearer[2] joined us.

Write the second footnote. Proceed just as with the first one. This time, place the cursor behind 'Alan Shearer'.

Recently I was in Stratford
Alan Shearer[joined us.

Place the cursor behind 'Alan Shearer'.

Yiew Inser\ Format

Open the INSERT menu.

Footnote...

Select the FOOTNOTE entry.

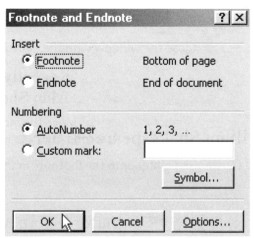

Confirm the entries with the *OK* button.

Footnotes | All Footnotes

¹ English poet
²|

5 The footnote window appears at the bottom of the screen.

Footnotes | All Footnotes ▾

¹ English poet
² English soccer player|

6 Enter the text of the second footnote.

Footnotes | All Footnotes ▾ | Close

¹ English poet
² English soccer player

7 Close the footnote window with the appropriate button.

Recently I was in Stratford
Alan Shearer² joined us.

8 Move the mouse pointer onto the second footnote in the text.

Recel English soccer player tratford
Alan Shearer² joined us.

9 The contents of the second footnote are displayed.

Deleting footnotes

Nothing is easier than deleting footnotes. Select the footnote you want to delete and press the ⟨Del⟩ key.

William Shakespeare[1]. Later

The result: not only has the footnote disappeared, but at the same time its contents have been deleted. But there is more! As soon as you delete a footnote, Word renumbers the remaining footnotes in their new order. The second footnote now becomes the first.

Shakespeare[1].

Select the first footnote.

Press the ⟨Del⟩ key.

William Shakespeare. Later

The footnote has been deleted.

Recently I was in Stratford Alan Shearer[1] joined us.

The second footnote is now the first.

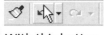

With this button you can undo the last command ...

6 # William Shakespeare‌. Later
... and restore the deleted footnote.

William Shakespeare[1]. Later

7 Unmark the selection with a mouse click anywhere in the document.

Viewing footnotes

Within the text footnotes are difficult to visualise. Apart from the superscript numbers you cannot see a thing.

You are still in **Normal** view. When you change the view and select **Print Layout**, the footnotes will be visible – use the scroll bar to get there – at the bottom of the page.

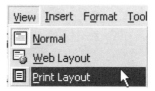

---

[1] English poet
[2] English soccer player

You can also view the footnotes by opening the **Print Preview**.

Move the magnifier to the bottom page margin and enlarge the view. After you have made sure that everything is correct, exit the print preview with the *Close* button or by pressing the [Esc] key.

Magnifier icon	When clicking the view is ...
	... reduced
	... enlarged

1 Click on the
Print Preview button.

¹ English poet
² English soccer player

2 Move the **magnifier** to the
footnotes at the bottom page
margin.

¹ English poet
² English soccer player

3 Enlarge the **view**.

4 Exit Print Peview with the
Close button or by pressing the
[Esc] key.

Inserting page numbers

He asked her, and immediately realised how keen she was, otherwise she would hardly have given her phone number, and he thought how stupid he had been waiting so long.

"She said with a smile.

8

In this example you have only one page.

Page numbers make more sense if your document consists of several pages.

Page numbering is the consecutive numbering of a set of pages.

In the INSERT menu select the PAGE NUMBERS command.

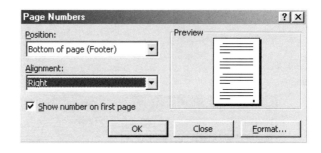

Here you specify where you want the numbers to appear: left, right, or centred on the paper.

Page numbers need not necessarily be inserted only at the bottom of the page. They can also be inserted at the top.

In the preview the black dot indicates where the page number will appear, as soon as you confirm this with the *OK* button.

By clicking on the *Format* button, you may also specify different types of numbering.

Page numbering may begin with any number. Select the *Format* button. Under *Start at*, enter the required number.

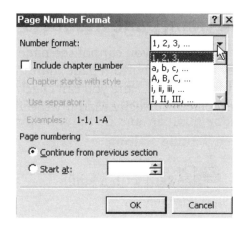

1 Open the INSERT menu.

2 **Page Numbers**

Select the PAGE NUMBERS command.

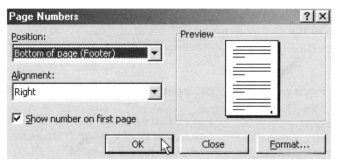

3 Confirm with the *OK* button.

Checking page numbers

In normal view you cannot see page numbers at all. In Print Layout they are on the bottom page margin. Once more, **Print Preview** turns out to be useful. Here you can check whether the page numbers have been placed correctly. Magnify the view with the magnifier.

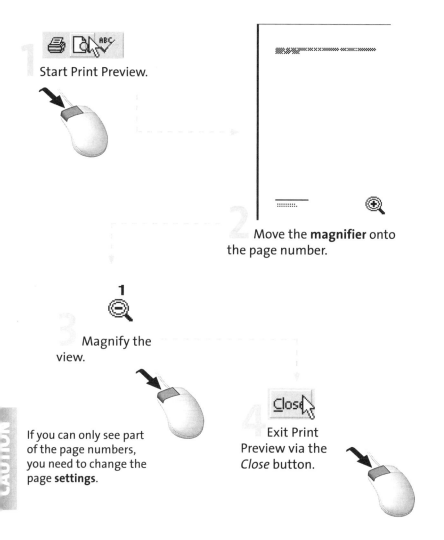

Start Print Preview.

Move the **magnifier** onto the page number.

1

Magnify the view.

If you can only see part of the page numbers, you need to change the page **settings**.

Exit Print Preview via the *Close* button.

This goes to show you how sensible it is to check the future print-out in **Print Preview**.

Changing page margins

Can you only see part of your page numbers? This means that this would also be the case in a future print-out. You need to change your document setup.

The Page Setup option of the File menu allows you to specify the **page margins** of your documents.

Word applies a default setting. When you increase the space for the footer, the page numbers will appear correctly.

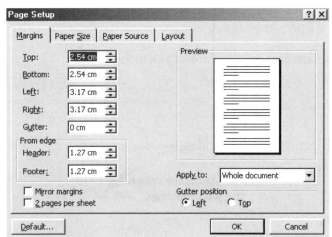

Change your settings if you need to. With the *Default* button you can specify that your own settings are to be taken as the new default settings from now on.

Practise, practise ... and practise again!

Carry out the individual steps on your own.

John Diver dived at the coast of Flaminguna. Suddenly he faced three sharks. He escaped from two, but not from the third.|

Enter the sample sentence above.
If necessary, change to normal view.

John Diver[1] dived at the coast of Flaminguna[2]. Suddenly he faced three sharks[3]. from two, but not from the third.

Create footnotes for the words 'Diver', 'Flaminguna', and 'sharks'.

Footnotes | All Footnotes | ▼ | Close

[1] British marine biologist
[2] One of the Acribic Islands
[3] Species of fish

Write the text into the footnotes window.

the coast of Flaminguna[2]. Suddenly

Select the second footnote.

John Diver[1] dived at the coast of Flaminguna. Suddenly he faced three sharks[2]. He escaped from two, but not from the third.

Delete it by pressing the [Del] key.

297

15

What's in this chapter:

If you are drowning and you can't swim properly, there is only one hope: you need a rescuer who will pull you out. However, if there is nobody, do you pray for a lifebelt? Word 2000 offers you lifebelts in form of numerous help programs. If things don't work out you can sit and pray for a miracle. Alternatively you can use the help features provided by Word. There are more of them than you might think!

The Assistant – with a little help from a friend

One additional feature of Word is the amusing Assistant animations that are available to you. When you click on the *Help* button, the **Assistant** appears on the screen.

Click on the *Help* button.

An Assistant appears on the screen.

You also activate the Assistant by pressing the F1 key.

This is 'Clippit', the vivacious paperclip. When you move the mouse pointer on the Assistant and press the **right mouse** button, a context menu opens.

Move the mouse pointer onto the Assistant.

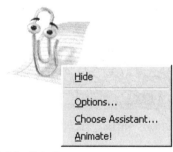

Right-click it.

From here you can get to various points.

Select the ANIMATE! entry, and the Assistant will give you a little performance. Activate it with the left mouse button (this is how the chapter opening illustrations of this book have been created).

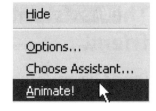

When you click on CHOOSE ASSISTANT, a varied choice of helpers appears. With the *Next* and *Back* buttons you can view them one by one. As well as the four characters shown below, there are many others.

The choice is all yours. If you decide to **change Assistant** you will need to insert the Office 2000 installation CD. Confirm the selected Assistant with *OK*.

Under OPTIONS, you specify which kind of tips you want your Assistant to display.

Click on the *Options* entry.

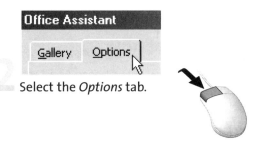

Select the *Options* tab.

Here you can specify how you want the Assistant to offer its help. The options are assigned by default.

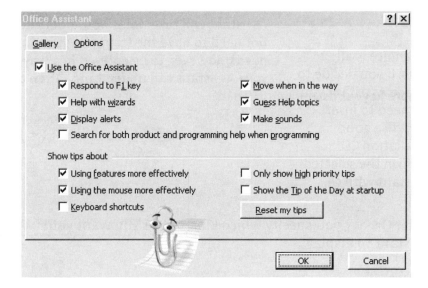

Under *Show tips about* you can extend the tips. You can, for example, select the *Keyboard shortcuts* option to instruct the Assistant to show you tips about key combinations.

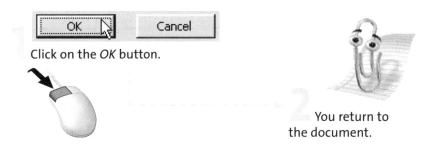

Click on the *OK* button.

You return to the document.

301

Who, how, what? If you don't ask you don't get!

While you are working the assistant will be there for you and put forward suggestions.

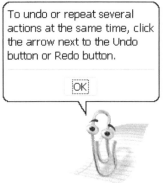

To undo or repeat several actions at the same time, click the arrow next to the Undo button or Redo button.

OK

Whenever you have a question about Word simply click on your Assistant. Enter your query, and then click on the *Search* button. While you are phrasing your question, your Assistant will take notes. Your query does not need to have the form of a question. It needs, however, to be entered in a way your Assistant can understand. Often **one or more keywords** will be sufficient.

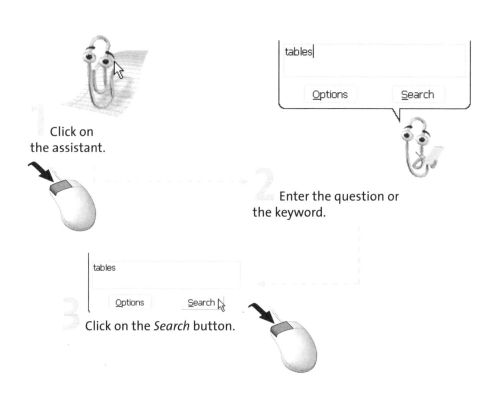

Click on the assistant.

tables|

Options   Search

Enter the question or the keyword.

tables

Options   Search

Click on the *Search* button.

You will be offered several options, which may be relevant, as a solution. Select the most relevant option. Word offers you information and instructions connected with the topic.

What would you like to do?

○ Abouttables

○ Create a table

○ Office programs you can use to create a table

○ Troubleshoot tables

○ Add rows or columns to a table

▼ See more…

tables

Select a topic with a mouse click.

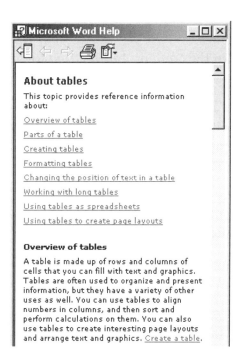

Word Help opens on your screen.

In this help function you can look up individual topics. By pressing the
 button, everything can be printed out so that you have a hard
copy for the future.

By using the arrow buttons you can move back and forth
through the various help topics.

303

1 Click on the button shown above.

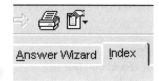

2 Word Help is expanded on your screen.

On the *Contents* tab you find the individual help books. Double-click on a book, and a selection of individual topics is displayed.

If you activate the *Answer Wizard* tab with a mouse click, you can enter your questions or keywords under *What would you like to do?*

As soon as you click on the *Search* button, Word comes up with suggestions.

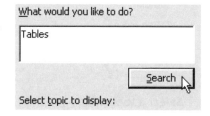

You can enter keywords with which you need help on the *Index* tab. When you enter your first keyword under *1. Type keywords*, you will

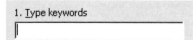

notice that Word jumps further and further down the list of keywords shown underneath each time a new letter is entered. Thus Word Help already selects terms which might become relevant.

Close Word Help by clicking on the *Close* button (the little X) on the title bar.

What's this?

A help function everybody should know about is 'What's This?'

In the *Help* menu click...

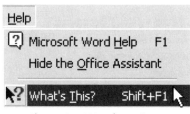

... on the entry WHAT'S THIS?

Your mouse pointer becomes an arrow with a question mark.

You can also activate **What's This?** with the ⬆+F1 keyboard shortcut.

You are now provided with an extensive **description** instead of the usual ScreenTips. Deactivate *What's this?* with the Esc key.

Even within a **dialog box** you will find additional help. When you click on the question mark at the right hand end of the title bar a question mark is added to your mouse pointer.

When you click on any element in the dialog box, you will now receive the required information. Click anywhere on the screen, and the description disappears.

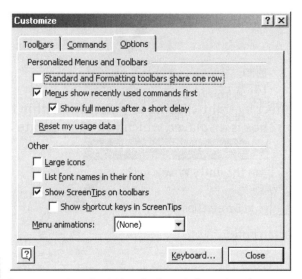

For example select the *Options* tab under the
TOOLS/CUSTOMIZE menu option.

Click on the question mark on the title bar of the dialog box.

A question mark appears at the mouse pointer.

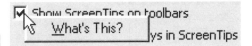

4 When you click on any option within the dialog
box, the corresponding description is displayed.

You achieve the same effect by **right-clicking** any element within the
dialog box. A *What's This?* box is displayed which you can activate by
clicking on it.

With a right-click, select an option.

Left-click on *What's This?*

The **Assistant**
too can be
called from
within a dialog box.

Bye! See you in
the next Word!

307

Solutions

Chapter 3

Exercise I

Decide whether these statements are (t)rue or (f)alse.

(f) If you adopt the word 'mistake', you correct all misspelled words.

(t) With *Add* this mistake will be ignored in all future documents.

(f) With *Ignore All* this mistake will be ignored in all future documents.

Chapter 6

Clicking on the *Open* button and the FILE/OPEN menu option leads ...

❏ to different dialog boxes.

☒ to the *Open* dialog box.

❏ to the *Save* dialog box.

When assigning a password for read- and write-protection, the case of the password is ...

☒ important

❑ unimportant

A document can only be deleted ...

❑ when it is opened on the screen.

☒ when it is not opened on the screen.

Quick text selection with the mouse

Good morning!

The toaster is ringing. I rub my eyes, slowly waking up, and have a shower. Ouch, the water is piping hot! The eggs are boiling. Where's the towel? I put on the coffee and wake up the kids. Then I take them to school. Damn! I haven't got any kids. My wife's on the pill. I drive home, get dressed, eat the coffee and drink a toast. The butter's hard as a rock. No jam in the fridge either. But yesterday it was there. I dig out a bar of chocolate from last Christmas. Chocolate on toast: it's good for nerves. I'd like to brush my teeth, but how? I can't find the toothbrush. A mouthwash will have to do for today. Always chaos this early in the morning. Who cares! I'll take the car and drive to work. But I haven't got a car! OK, for once, the neighbour will have to take the train. I'm the first one in the office; that has never happened before. Being still alone after an hour, I'm getting suspicious. Something must be wrong! I look at the calendar! Today's Friday, a normal working day. I ask the porter. He says the whole crowd is out on a corporate excursion. A barbecue on the lake! I look out of the window. It's winter. I rush down to the lake, crossing a red traffic light. A flash of light hits my eyes. Once on the lake's shore, nobody's there, except a couple of ducks who look quiet alive and not barbecued at all. I drive back to work and blow the office block to pieces. Back home, I wait for the police. But they don't arrive. I decide to have another couple of hours' sleep before I get arrested, so I can be fresh for the interrogation.
The alarm clock rings. My wife, waking up next to me, gives me a kiss. "Morning, dear, today's Sunday and we can sleep in!"
"Yes" says I and stop the alarm clock. It was only a dream!
And I stretch leisurely while downstairs the police are pulling into my driveway.

With a mouse click anywhere in the document you can **deselect** a **selection** again.

Selecting characters, text sections or the whole document is often done much more quickly with the mouse. You just have to know how to do it!

Selecting a word

Good·morning!¶
¶
The·toaster·is·ringing.·

1 Point the mouse to a word.

Good·morning!¶
¶
The· toaster is·ringing.·

2 Double-click it with the left mouse button.

Selecting a whole line

The toaster is ringi
is piping hot! The
kids. Then I take tl
home, get dressed,
fridge either. But y

1 Position the mouse pointer **in front of a line**, until it turns into an arrow which tilts slightly to the right.

The·toaster·is·ringi
is·piping·hot!·The·
kids.·Then·I·take·tl
home,·get·dressed,
fridge·either.·But·y

2 Left-click once in front of the line.

Selecting several lines at a time

Chocolate on toast: it's good for nerves.
toothbrush. A mouthwash will have to d

1 Place the mouse pointer in front of a line.

311

> Chocolate on toast: it's good
> toothbrush. A mouthwash w
> Who cares! I'll take the car a
> neighbour will have to take t

2 Keeping the left button pressed, drag the mouse downwards to select several lines.

Selecting a sentence

1 Keeping the [Ctrl] key pressed ...

2 The bu**t**ter's hard as a rock.
... click **inside a sentence**.

3 1st. The butter's hard as a rock. No
The sentence is now selected.

Selecting a paragraph

> fridge either. But yeste
> Chocolate on toast: it's
> toothbrush. A mouthw
> Who cares! I'll take th
> neighbour will have to
> before. Being still alor
> look at the calendar! T
> whole crowd is out on

1 Place the mouse pointer **in front of any line of the paragraph.**

Good morning!

The toaster is ringing. I rub my eyes, slowly waking up, and have a shower. Ouch, the water is piping hot! The eggs are boiling. Where's the towel? I put on the coffee and wake up the kids. Then I take them to school. Damn! I haven't got any kids. My wife's on the pill. I drive home, get dressed, eat the coffee and drink a toast. The butter's hard as a rock. No jam in the fridge either. But yesterday it was there. I dig out a bar of chocolate from last Christmas. Chocolate on toast: it's good for nerves. I'd like to brush my teeth, but how? I can't find the toothbrush. A mouthwash will have to do for today. Always chaos this early in the morning. Who cares! I'll take the car and drive to work. But I haven't got a car! Ok, for once, the neighbour will have to take the train. I'm the first one in the office; that has never happened before. Being still alone after an hour, I'm getting suspicious. Something must be wrong! I look at the calendar! Today's Friday, a normal working day. I ask the porter. He says the whole crowd is out on a corporate excursion. A barbecue on the lake! I look out of the window. It's winter. I rush down to the lake, crossing a red traffic light. A flash of light hits my eyes. Once on the lake's shore, nobody's there, except a couple of ducks who look quiet alive and not barbecued at all. I drive back to work and blow the office block to pieces. Back home, I wait for the police. But they don't arrive. I decide to have another couple of hours sleep before I get arrested, so I can be fresh for the interrogation.

The alarm clock rings. My wife, waking up next to me, gives me a kiss. "Morning, dear, today's Sunday and we can sleep in!"

"Yes" says I and stop the alarm clock. It was only a dream!

And I stretch leisurely while downstairs the police are pulling into my driveway.

Double-click.

Selecting a large amount of text

The toaster is ringing. I rub
is piping hot! The eggs are l
kids. Then I take them to sc
home, get dressed, eat the c
fridge either. But yesterday

Click at the point where the
selection is supposed to start.

Keeping the
key pressed ...

313

> The toaster is ringing. I rub my eyes, slowly waking up, and have a shower. Ouch, the ~~is piping hot! The eggs are boiling. Where's the towel? I put on the coffee and wake up~~ ~~kids. Then I take them to school. Damn! I haven't got any kids. My wife's on the pill. I~~ ~~home, get dressed, eat the coffee and drink a toast. The butter's hard as a rock.~~ No jam

... click on the required **end of the selection**.

Selecting the whole document

Open the EDIT menu.

Click on the SELECT ALL entry.

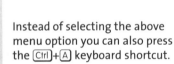

Instead of selecting the above menu option you can also press the ⌃tⁱl+Ⓐ keyboard shortcut.

Keyboard shortcuts

Instead of executing menu commands or clicking on buttons, you can call up the same commands in Word with the aid of keyboard shortcuts. Once you know them, you can access all of Word's functions IN NO TIME. Here is an extensive overview.

Command name	Modifiers	Key
All Caps	Ctrl + ⇧ +	A
Annotation	Alt + Ctrl +	M
Apply List Bullet	Ctrl + ⇧ +	L
Apply Maximize	Alt +	F10
Apply Restore	Alt +	F5
Auto Format	Alt + Ctrl +	K
Auto Text		F3
Auto Text	Alt + Ctrl +	V
Bold	Ctrl +	B
Bold	Ctrl + ⇧ +	B
Bookmark	Ctrl + ⇧ +	F5
Cancel		Esc
Change Case	⇧ +	F3
Character Left		←
Character Left Extend	⇧ +	←
Character Right		→
Character Right Extend	⇧ +	→
Clear		Del
Close All	Alt +	A
Close or Exit	Alt +	F4
Close Pane	Alt + ⇧ +	C
Column Break	Ctrl + ⇧ +	↵

Command name	Modifiers	Key
Copy Format	Ctrl + ⇧ +	C
Copy Text	⇧ +	F2
Copy	Ctrl +	C
Copy	Ctrl +	Ins
Create AutoText	Alt +	F3
Customize Add Menu Shortcut	Alt + Ctrl + ⇧ +	0
Customize Keyboard Shortcut	Alt + Ctrl +	Num +
Customize Remove Menu Shortcut	Alt + Ctrl +	-
Cut	Ctrl +	X
Cut	⇧ +	Del
Date Field	Alt + ⇧ +	D
Delete Back Word	Ctrl +	⬅
Delete Word	Ctrl +	Del
Dictionary	Alt + ⇧ +	F7
Do Field Click	Alt + ⇧ +	F9
Document Close	Ctrl +	F4
Document Close	Ctrl +	W
Document Maximize	Ctrl +	F10
Document Move	Ctrl +	F7
Document Restore	Ctrl +	F5
Document Size	Ctrl +	F8
Document Split	Alt + Ctrl +	S
Double Underline	Ctrl + ⇧ +	D
End of Column	Alt +	Pg↓
End of Column	Alt + ⇧ +	Pg↓
End of Document	Ctrl +	End
End of Document Extend	Ctrl + ⇧ +	End
End of Line		End

Command name	Modifiers	Key
End of Line Extend	⇧+	End
End of Row	Alt+	End
End of Row	Alt+⇧+	End
End of Window	Alt+Ctrl+	Pg↓
End of Window Extend	Alt+Ctrl+⇧+	Pg↓
Endnote Now	Alt+Ctrl+	D
Field Characters	Ctrl+	F9
Field Codes	Alt+	F9
Find	Ctrl+	F
Font Size Select	Ctrl+⇧+	P
Font	Ctrl+	D
Font	Ctrl+⇧+	F
Footnote Now	Alt+Ctrl+	F
Go Back	Alt+Ctrl+	Z
Go Back	⇧+	F5
Go To		F5
Go To	Ctrl+	G
Grow Font One Point	Alt+Ctrl+	9
Hanging Indent	Ctrl+	T
Header Footer Link	Alt+⇧+	R
Help		F1
Hidden	Ctrl+⇧+	H
Hyperlink	Ctrl+	K
Indent	Ctrl+	M
Italic	Ctrl+	I
Italic	Ctrl+⇧+	I
Line Down		↓
Line Down Extend	⇧+	↓

317

Command name	Modifiers	Key
Line Spacing 1	Ctrl +	1
Line Spacing 1.5	Ctrl +	5
Line Spacing 2	Ctrl +	2
Line Up		↑
Line Up Extend	⇧ +	↑
List Num Field	Alt + Ctrl +	L
Lock Fields	Ctrl +	3
Lock Fields	Ctrl +	F11
Macro	Alt +	F8
Mail Merge Check	Alt + ⇧ +	K
Mail Merge Edit Data Source	Alt + ⇧ +	E
Mail Merge to Doc	Alt + ⇧ +	N
Mail Merge to Printer	Alt + ⇧ +	M
Mark Citation	Alt + ⇧ +	I
Mark Index Entry	Alt + ⇧ +	X
Mark Table of Contents Entry	Alt + ⇧ +	O
Menu Mode		F10
Merge Field	Alt + ⇧ +	F
Microsoft Script Editor	Alt + ⇧ +	F11
Microsoft System Info	Alt + Ctrl +	F1
Move Text		F2
New	Ctrl +	N
Next Cell		⇥
Next Field		F11
Next Field	Alt +	F1
Next Misspelling	Alt +	F7
Next Object	Alt +	↓
Next Window	Alt +	F6

Command name	Modifiers	Key
Next Window	`Ctrl`+	`F6`
Normal Style	`Alt`+`⇧`+	`Num` `5`
Normal Style	`Ctrl`+`⇧`+	`N`
Normal	`Alt`+`Ctrl`+	`N`
Open or Close Up Para	`Ctrl`+	`0`
Open	`Alt`+`Ctrl`+	`F2`
Open	`Ctrl`+	`F12`
Open	`Ctrl`+	`O`
Other Pane		`F6`
Other Pane	`⇧`+	`F6`
Outline Collapse	`Alt`+`⇧`+	`-`
Outline Collapse	`Alt`+`⇧`+	`Num` `-`
Outline Demote	`Alt`+`⇧`+	`→`
Outline Expand	`Alt`+`⇧`+	`+`
Outline Expand	`Alt`+`⇧`+	`Num` `+`
Outline MoveDown	`Alt`+`⇧`+	`↓`
Outline Move Up	`Alt`+`⇧`+	`↑`
Outline Promote	`Alt`+`⇧`+	`←`
Outline Show First Line	`Alt`+`⇧`+	`L`
Outline	`Alt`+`Ctrl`+	`O`
Overtype		`Ins`
Page	`Alt`+`Ctrl`+	`P`
Page Break	`Ctrl`+	`↵`
Page Down		`Pg↓`
Page Down Extend	`⇧`+	`Pg↓`
Page Field	`Alt`+`⇧`+	`P`
Page Up		`Pg↑`
Page Up Extend	`⇧`+	`Pg↑`

319

Command name	Modifiers	Key
Paragraph Center	Ctrl +	E
Paragraph Down	Ctrl +	↓
Paragraph Down Extend	Ctrl + ⇧ +	↓
Paragraph Justify	Ctrl +	J
Paragraph Left	Ctrl +	L
Paragraph Right	Ctrl +	R
Paragraph Up	Ctrl +	↑
Paragraph Up Extend	Ctrl + ⇧ +	↑
Paste	Ctrl +	V
Paste	⇧ +	Ins
Paste Format	Ctrl + ⇧ +	V
Previous Cell	⇧ +	⇥
Previous Field	Alt + ⇧ +	F1
Previous Field	⇧ +	F11
Previous Object	Alt +	↑
Previous Window	Alt + ⇧ +	F6
Previous Window	Ctrl + ⇧ +	F6
Print Preview	Alt + Ctrl +	I
Print Preview	Ctrl +	F2
Print	Ctrl +	P
Print	Ctrl + ⇧ +	F12
Proofing		F7
Redo or Repeat		F4
Redo or Repeat	Alt +	↵
Redo or Repeat	Ctrl +	Y
Redo	Alt + ⇧ +	⇐
Repeat Find	Alt + Ctrl +	Y
Repeat Find	⇧ +	F4

Command name	Modifiers	Key
Replace	Ctrl +	H
Reset Char	Ctrl +	⬯
Reset Char	Ctrl + ⇧ +	Z
Reset Para	Ctrl +	Q
Revision Marks Toggle	Ctrl + ⇧ +	E
Save	Alt + ⇧ +	F2
Save	Ctrl +	S
Save	⇧ +	F12
Save As		F12
Select All	Ctrl +	A
Select All	Ctrl +	Num 5
Select Column	Ctrl + ⇧ +	F8
Select Table	Alt +	Num 5
Selection Extend		F8
Selection Shrink	⇧ +	F8
Show All	Ctrl + ⇧ +	8
Shrink Font One Point	Alt + Ctrl +	8
Shrink Font	Ctrl + ⇧ +	<
Small Caps	Ctrl + ⇧ +	K
Spike	Ctrl +	F3
Spike	Ctrl + ⇧ +	F3
Start of Column	Alt +	Pg↑
Start of Column	Alt + ⇧ +	Pg↑
Start of Document	Ctrl +	Home
Start of Document Extend	Ctrl + ⇧ +	Home
Start of Line		Home
Start of Line Extend	⇧ +	Home
Start of Row	Alt +	Home

Command name	Modifiers	Key
Start of Row	Alt+⇧+	Home
Start of Window	Alt+Ctrl+	Pg↑
Start of Window Extend	Alt+Ctrl+⇧+	Pg↑
Style	Ctrl+⇧+	S
Subscript	Ctrl+⇧+	0
Superscript	Ctrl+	+
Symbol Font	Ctrl+⇧+	Q
Thesaurus	⇧+	F7
Time Field	Alt+⇧+	T
Toggle Field Display	⇧+	F9
Toggle Master Subdocs	Alt+Ctrl+	\
Tool	⇧+	F1
Un Hang	Ctrl+⇧+	T
Un Indent	Ctrl+⇧+	M
Underline	Ctrl+	U
Underline	Ctrl+⇧+	U
Undo	Alt+	⇦
Undo	Ctrl+	Z
Word Left	Ctrl+	←
Word Left Extend	Ctrl+⇧+	←
Word Right	Ctrl+	→
Word Right Extend	Ctrl+⇧+	→
Word Underline	Ctrl+⇧+	W

What are all those keys for?

The `Alt` key

Abbbreviation for 'Alternate Key'. This key is used to activate the meu bar in Windows programs. Furthermore, the `Alt` key is often a part of keyboard shortcuts. The third alternative: pressing `Alt` and a number on the numeric keypad generates a character.

The `⇧` key

The largest area of the keyboard is the 'alphanumeric' keyboard. Its handling is practically identical to that of a typewriter keyboard. You will find nearly all of the functions you already know from your typewriter, for example the `⇧` key (= Shift key).

This key is used for typing single upper case characters. First you press the `⇧` key and, keeping it pressed, type the required character.

Example

Above the number 5 on the alphanumeric keyboard you will find the % sign. Keeping the `⇧` key pressed, type the 5. The % sign appears.

In this way, you type all the characters that can be found on keys showing two characters one above the other.

Try to type in: 'A & O Ltd'

Some more exercises

36 °

§ 367

15 * 3 = 45

Asterix Volume XXVII

5 > 4

The CapsLock key ⟨⇩⟩

HERE ALL LETTERS ARE WRITTEN IN UPPER CASE!

Tip: The CapsLock indicator at the top right corner of your keyboard lights up.

The function is switched off by pressing the ⟨⇧⟩ key again.

Alternate characters

Some keys show a third character (on non-English keyboards, there are quite a lot of them, while on the most recent English Windows keyboards, we just find the vertical bar on the top left key and the Euro symbol next to the 4). To obtain these characters, press the ⟨Alt Gr⟩ key. Keeping it pressed, type the required character.

The ⟨↵⟩ key (= Enter/Return key)

Another important key is the ⟨↵⟩ key. This is used to tell the computer to start processing the freshly entered command.

The ⟨▭▭⟩ bar

Because of its shape, this key is usually called 'Space bar' (not 'key'). Pressing it once creates a blank space.

The ⟨⇦⟩ key

Assume you would like to type the word 'mistake'.

Thus you type ...

mit	and realise you have made a mistake. Now you press the ⬅ key.
mi_	The incorrect 't' has been deleted.
mistake_	Now you can go on typing correctly.

The numeric keypad

At the very right of your keyboard you will find the so-called numeric keypad.

You switch it on and off with the (Num) key. When it is switched on, the 'NumLock' indicator on your keyboard automatically lights up.

The numeric keypad is very useful, for example, for entering numbers into a table on your screen.

The cursor keys ⬅, ⬆, ➡, ⬇

Between the alphanumeric and the numeric pad, you will find the cursor or arrow pad. Its keys are used to move the cursor across the screen.

The function keys

Above the alphanumeric keyboard, you can see the function keys (F1) to (F12). These keys do not generate characters on your screen, but trigger a function or a process. What happens when you press a function key depends on the program currently in use.

Insert mode

Characters you insert at any position are inserted; the remaining characters are shifted to the right. This mode is switched on and off with the (Ins) key.

Overwrite mode

Newly typed in characters overwrite characters that have already been entered. This mode is switched on and off with the (Ins) key.

Keyboard overview

Key name	Term	Function	Key symbol
Alt		Depends on the program in use	⟨Alt⟩
Alt Gr		Alternative key characters	⟨Alt Gr⟩
Backspace	Backward delete	Deletes the most recently entered character	⟨⇦⟩
CapsLock	Permanent shift	Permanent upper case characters	⟨⬇⟩
Ctrl	Control	Depending on the program in combination with another key	⟨Ctrl⟩
Cursor keys	Arrow keys	Cursor movement	⟨←⟩ ⟨↑⟩ ⟨↓⟩ ⟨→⟩
Del	Forward delete	Deletes a character to the right of the cursor	⟨Del⟩
End		Cursor jumps to end of line	⟨End⟩
Escape		Terminates a function	⟨Esc⟩
Function keys		Trigger specific functions or processes	⟨F1⟩ to ⟨F12⟩
Home		Cursor jumps back to the first (Home) position	⟨Home⟩
Ins	Insert	Inserts characters to the right of the cursor	⟨Ins⟩
NumLock	Numeric keypad	Activates the numeric keypad	⟨Num⟩
Pause	Break	Stops/freezes the screen	⟨Pause⟩
Pg Dn		Next screen contents	⟨Bild ↓⟩
Pg Up		Previous screen contents	⟨Bild ↑⟩

Key name	Term	Function	Key symbol
Print		Screen print-out	`Print`
Return key	Enter/Return ley	Confirms a command input	`⏎`
Shift key		Upper case characters	`⇧`
Spacebar		Blank space	`▭`
Tab	Tab stop	Moves the insertion point to the next tab position	`⇆`

327

Getting to grips with Word

The Title bar

The Title bar tells you which document you are currently working on. Imagine a document as something like a piece of (type)written matter consisting of one or more pages.

Documents are given a name. In Word, this is done with the Save command **(Chapter 5).**

The word **Document** in the Title bar means that nothing has been saved yet. It is a name which is automatically assigned by Word.

![Document1 - Microsoft Word]

The number **1** after 'Document' informs you that you are currently working on your first document on screen.

Once you have saved a document, its name appears in the Title bar.

(Chapter 5)

![Exercise.doc - Microsoft Word]

The Menu bar

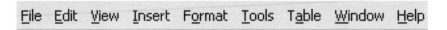

In the Menu bar you can call up the most varied commands, such as Open, Save, Print or Exit.

To do this, you first open a menu option by clicking on it with the left mouse button and then select the required entry in the opened menu.

(Chapter 2)

Examples:

➟ FILE/OPEN ...

➟ EDIT/COPY

➟ VIEW/TOOLBARS

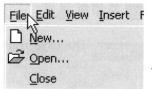

You can also access the Menu bar via the keyboard, where you can use the arrow keys to move around.

You access the menu with the ⎇Alt⎇ and ➔ keys . (A tip for handling this: first press and release the ⎇Alt⎇ key, then press the right cursor key ➔.)

Use the ←, ↑, ↓ and ➔ cursor keys to move around in the menu.

With the Esc key you deactivate the Menu bar.

329

The Standard toolbar

The Standard toolbar hosts the buttons (or icons) which represent frequently used commands you can also execute via the Menu bar.

A **button** in the toolbars is a sort of placeholder for a function (for example the outline of a printer for printing).

The essential advantage of the Standard toolbar against the Menu bar is that you can launch the individual commands more quickly with the mouse.

(Chapter 2)

New Blank Document

This is the button to use when you want to open a new document. A 'new blank document' means that you will get a new, empty document not yet worked upon.

(Chapter 3)

Open

The process of accessing an existing document is called 'Opening' or 'Loading' the document. To do this, you click on the *Open* button or select the FILE/OPEN menu item. In both cases, the same dialog box will open. In *Look in* you specify where the document is located. For a **diskette** you click on '3 1/2 Floppy (A:)'.

(Chapter 6)

Save

Everything you create and save with a Windows program such as Word or Excel becomes a file. To create files with Word you can either use the *Save* button or the FILE/SAVE or FILE/SAVE AS commands.

You save a document in order to store it permanently on your computer's hard disk. In *Save in* you specify where you want to store the document. Word automatically proposes the 'My Documents' folder. However, you can specify any other location on the hard drive or a floppy disk.

The **hard disk** is usually a built-in storage medium in your computer which allows the storage of large amounts of data even when the computer is switched off.

If you save to a **diskette,** click on '3 1/2 Floppy (A:)'.

(Chapter 5)

E-mail

'Mail' the electronic way. You can send your document via the Internet.

Print

To see your text in black on white, you can print it out. Printing is carried out from the printer set up in Windows. With the FILE/ PRINT menu option, you specify which pages, how many copies, the range etc. you want to print.

(Chapter 5)

Print Preview

You will find Print Preview under the command in the FILE menu. You can access it more quickly with the button in the Standard toolbar.

One click, and you are in Print Preview, that is, the preview of how a future print-out would look.

(Chapter 5 and 14)

Spelling and Grammar

A click on this button checks the document for possible spelling mistakes.

(Chapter 3)

Cut

You cut something out, the original disappears and can be inserted at a different point.

(Chapter 7)

Copy

Copying is very much like cutting. When you cut something, the original disappears; whereas, when you copy, the original stays as it is.

(Chapter 7)

Paste

A mouse click on this button inserts the contents of the clipboard. Data are transferred onto the clipboard, for example, after you have clicked on the *Cut* or *Copy* button.

(Chapter 7)

Format Painter

Clicking this button once with the left mouse button changes the shape of the mouse pointer into a paintbrush as soon as you position it over the document. If you want to transfer a format more than once, double-click on this button.

'Paintbrush' button	Effect
Single-click	You can transfer the format once.

'Paintbrush' button	Effect
Double-click	You can transfer the **format any number** of times.
Press the [Esc] key or click the 'Paintbrush' button again. (Chapter 7)	The function is switched off.

Undo

This button undoes the action you performed most recently. With each click, a further action is undone.
(Chapter 7, 12 and 14)

Redo

If you want to carry out an undone action again, you click on the *Redo* button.

Insert Hyperlink

Inserts a link (reference), for example, to another file.

Tables and Borders

 With the aid of a table pencil you can design your own tables. You can either use the TABLE/DRAW TABLE menu option or click on the *Tables and borders* button.

Whichever way you choose, an additional toolbar appears on your screen, which gives you access to a number of features for laying out and designing tables and borders.
(Chapter 12)

Insert Table

To create a table you choose the TABLE/INSERT/TABLE menu option and subsequently enter the number of rows and columns.

A quicker way of doing this is to click on the *Insert Table* button.

When you click on the button, a submenu appears in which you specify the size – that is, the number of rows and columns – of the table.
(Chapter 12)

Insert Microsoft Excel Worksheet

Inserts a Microsoft worksheet created in the Excel program at the position of the insertion point.

Columns

Changes the number of columns in a document. When you click on the button, a submenu appears in which you specify the desired number of columns.

Drawing

Clicking on this button shows/hides the Drawing toolbar.
(Chapter 8 and 11)

Document Map

Shows/hides the document map view. The document map is a vertical section displayed on the left of the document window which gives you an overview of the structure of the document. You use the document map for quickly scrolling through a long document or a Web document without losing the overall view.

Show/Hide Formatting Marks

This button is used to show the formatting marks.
(Chapter 2)

Formatting mark		Meaning	Keys
· · · · · · · · · ·		Spaces	⌷
¶		Paragraph mark	↵
↵		End of line	⇧ + ↵
→	→	Tab stops	⇥

Zoom

With Word's Zoom function you increase or
reduce the view of the current document.
(Chapter 2)

Word Help

When you click on the ? button, an Assistant appears.
(Chapter 15)

More Buttons

In Word, you can add and remove buttons as you wish. In the
Standard toolbar you will find the *More Buttons* button on the
extreme right. Clicking on it opens the *Add or Remove Buttons*
command.
(Chapter 13)

1 In the toolbar, click on the *More Buttons* button.

Add or Remove Bu~ons ▾

2 Move the mouse pointer onto the *Add or Remove Buttons* button.

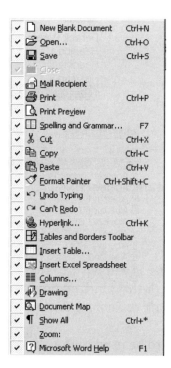

✓	🗋	New **B**lank Document	Ctrl+N
✓	📂	**O**pen...	Ctrl+O
✓	🖫	**S**ave	Ctrl+S
✓		Close	
✓	🖃	**M**ail Recipient	
✓	🖨	**P**rint	Ctrl+P
✓	🔍	Print Pre**v**iew	
✓	🔳	**S**pelling and Grammar...	F7
✓	✂	Cu**t**	Ctrl+X
✓	📋	**C**opy	Ctrl+C
✓	📋	**P**aste	Ctrl+V
✓	✍	**F**ormat Painter	Ctrl+Shift+C
✓	↼	**U**ndo Typing	
✓	↽	Can't **R**edo	
✓	🔗	H**y**perlink...	Ctrl+K
✓	⊞	**T**ables and Borders Toolbar	
✓	⬜	**I**nsert Table...	
✓	🔲	Insert Excel Spreadsheet	
✓	▦	**C**olumns...	
✓	⟨⟩	**D**rawing	
✓	🔍	**D**ocument Map	
✓	¶	**S**how All	Ctrl+*
✓		**Z**oom:	
✓	⟨?⟩	Microsoft Word **H**elp	F1

3 With the aid of the entries shown in the list, you can add or remove buttons to or from the Standard toolbar with a click of the mouse.

If a tick mark is shown in front of an entry, the corresponding button is already present on the Standard toolbar.

The Formatting toolbar

With the aid of this toolbar you can carry out formatting operations. You can, for example, choose a different font or highlight text in bold face or by underlining.

(Chapter 2)

Style

Here you select a style which is assigned to a selected paragraph.

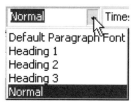

Font

This changes the current font or typeface. You may select any font from the list.

(Chapter 4)

Font Size

Here you can specify the size of the font to be used in the selected text. The displayed size depends on the font currently in use.

(Chapter 4)

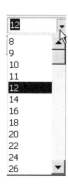

Formatting

Characters can be formatted in order to emphasise them visually. Most frequently, this is done by making the selected text bold, italic or underlined. Additional formatting options can be found on the *Font* tab under the FORMAT/FONT menu option.

(Chapter 4)

Aligning

The buttons *Align Left*, *Center* and *Align Right* are used to align a line or a paragraph to the left or the right margin of the document or to centre it between the margins.

The rightmost button you see here is used to *justify* text equally between the left and right margins. When you type from left to right, line lengths are usually different. Justified text makes the lines all of equal length. It is often found in books, newspapers and magazines.

(Chapter 4)

Numbering

This button adds numbering to a list or an enumeration. On the *Numbered* tab under the FORMAT/BULLETS AND NUMBERING menu option you can select additional ways of numbering.

(Chapter 8)

Decrease Indent/Increase Indent

Changes the position of the selected paragraph inside the document.

Outside Border

The selected text, paragraph or cell range of a table is assigned a border consisting of one or more border lines in different widths. If you want to remove a border line, select the *No Border* option from the *Border* palette.

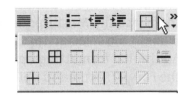

Font Colour

The colour palette gives you the choice of various colours in the form of small colour boxes. You can change the font colour or the colour of the background.

More buttons

In the Formatting toolbar you will find the *More Buttons* button at the extreme right. Clicking on it opens the *Add or Remove Buttons* command.

(Chapter 13)

1 In the Formatting toolbar, click on the *More Buttons* button.

2 Move the mouse pointer onto the *Add or Remove Buttons* button.

Add or Remove Button

✓		Style:	
✓		Font:	
✓		Font Size:	
✓	**B**	Bold	Ctrl+B
✓	*I*	Italic	Ctrl+I
✓	**U**	Underline	Ctrl+U
✓	≣	Align Left	Ctrl+L
✓	≣	Center	Ctrl+E
✓	≣	Align Right	Ctrl+R
✓	≣	Justify	Ctrl+J
✓	≣	Numbering	
✓	≣	Bullets	
✓	≣	Decrease Indent	
✓	≣	Increase Indent	
✓	☐	Borders	
✓	✎	Highlight	
✓	**A**	Font Color	
	=	Single Spacing	Ctrl+1
	=	1.5 Spacing	Ctrl+5
	=	Double Spacing	Ctrl+2
	x^2	Superscript	Ctrl++
	x_2	Subscript	Ctrl+=
		Language	

If a tick mark is shown in front of an entry, the corresponding button is already present on the Formatting toolbar. With the aid of these entries, you can add or remove buttons to or from the Formatting toolbar with a click of the mouse.

One row or not one row?

On the *Options* tab in the *Customize* dialog you will find entries which change the appearance of your screen in Word.

The Standard and Formatting toolbars can either share one row or be displayed one underneath the other.

(Chapter 13)

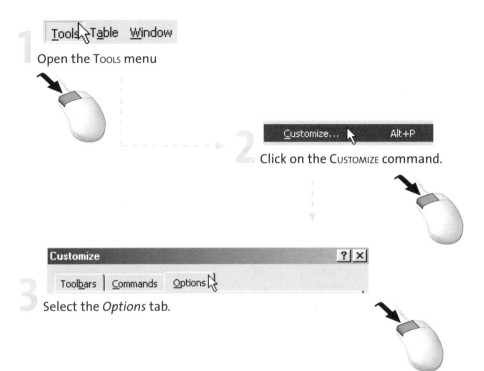

1 Open the Tools menu

2 Click on the Customize command.

3 Select the *Options* tab.

If you find a tick mark in front of the entry, click on it. This causes the toolbars to be displayed on two rows underneath each other.

(Chapters 2 and 13)

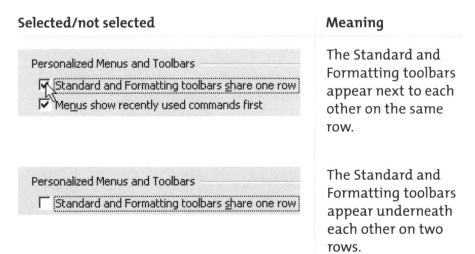

Selected/not selected	Meaning
Personalized Menus and Toolbars ☑ Standard and Formatting toolbars share one row ☑ Menus show recently used commands first	The Standard and Formatting toolbars appear next to each other on the same row.
Personalized Menus and Toolbars ☐ Standard and Formatting toolbars share one row	The Standard and Formatting toolbars appear underneath each other on two rows.

The Ruler

You can show or hide the ruler on your screen in two different ways.

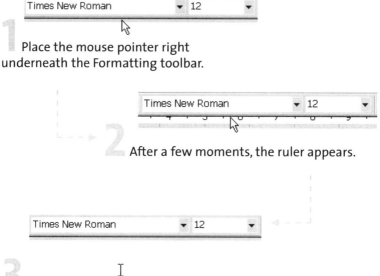

1 Place the mouse pointer right underneath the Formatting toolbar.

2 After a few moments, the ruler appears.

3 Move the mouse pointer back into the document. The ruler disappears from the screen.

The disadvantage of this procedure is that the ruler is not permanently displayed. On the other hand, however, this leaves more space for your document.

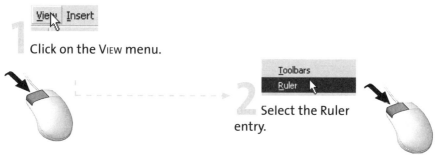

1 Click on the VIEW menu.

2 Select the Ruler entry.

From now on, the ruler is permanently displayed on your screen. You can hide it by unchecking the Ruler entry in the View menu.

(Chapter 12)

Glossary

Access protection

Only permits users who know the write/read password to open documents.

You can set up or edit access protection by activating the *Options* button when saving a document with the menu command FILE/SAVE AS. (Chapter 6)

Animations

Optical effects when clicking on the menu bar. These are switched on/off with the command VIEW/TOOLBARS/CUSTOMIZE on the tab Options.

Assistant

Assistants help with the execution of certain steps, and assist the user to solve similarly structured tasks. As in a manual the steps are outlined one

(Chapter 8)

AUTOEXEC.BAT

A special purpose batch file (*.BAT), which transmits important DOS commands to the computer at start-up. You can view and edit it in any editor. By means of this file and the file CONFIG.SYS you can analyse and remove memory and many other system problems.

Automatic hyphenation

See hyphenation.

AutoText

Frequently repeated phrases can be saved as AutoText and can then be called up in various documents, for example by typing in an abbreviation and hitting the [F3] key. (Chapter 10)

Baud

Baud is a measurement of the number of signal changes per second which can be processed by a modem.

Browser

A program with which you can use the WWW (World Wide Web) and display the data and the links of the Internet on your screen. The software is supplied by the Internet provider or the data service operator. However, it is also available directly from the Internet. Two of the most popular browsers are Microsoft Internet Explorer and Netscape Navigator.

Bug

A program fault which causes the computer to behave undesirably. The origin of the word derives from the first computer, ENIAC. A bug which got caught in its circuits caused faulty behaviour in the computer.

Buttons

1. Usually a component of dialog boxes. For example, you could confirm the selected options in a dialog box by clicking on the OK button. By clicking on the Cancel button you leave the dialog box without changing anything.

(Chapter 2)

2. A button on the toolbar represents a function (for example, the shape of a printer for printing).　　　　　　　　(Appendix 'Getting to grips with Word')

Byte

After bit, the second smallest unit of computer data. One byte is equivalent to a letter or character (see Megabyte).

Chat

A chat is the option of communicating live online with other participants. The conversation is carried out via the keyboard.

ClipArt

Word possesses a small library of ready–made images, the ClipArt Gallery.

(Chapter 11)

Clipboard

The clipboard is usually used by Windows to move or copy text. With the commands Copy or Cut the text is stored on the clipboard and can be inserted when required (with the Paste command). The contents are cleared if the computer is restarted.　　　　　　　　　　　　　　　　(Chapter 7)

Colour palette

The colour palette offers you a selection of various colours in the form of small colour boxes. A single mouse click on one of the boxes selects a colour.

Comment

A comment is a remark which is inserted into a text. Comments can be shown or hidden with the VIEW/COMMENTS command.

Component

Every type of hardware which is directly or indirectly connected to the computer.

Compression

A technique to reduce file size before archiving, transmitting or saving (see ZIP files).

Computer

From the word to compute (calculate).

Condition

An expression is formulated with a condition. A prerequisite for the execution of instructions which are assigned to this condition is that the expression is TRUE. If the expression is FALSE, the instructions are skipped or alternative instructions are carried out.   (Chapter 9)

CONFIG.SYS

A configuration file that transmits essential DOS memory and system commands to the computer at start-up. You can view and edit this file with any editor. By means of this file and the file AUTOEXEC.BAT you can analyse and remove memory and many other system problems (see AUTOEXEC.BAT).

Context menu

Right-clicking the mouse opens a context menu. The name refers to the fact that the composition of the individual menu items is dependent on the context or the situation in which the mouse button is pressed.   (Chapter 2)

CPI

Short for characters per inch. It is a unit of measurement for the character density in printers.   (Chapter 5)

Cursor

An on-screen position indicator in form of a flashing vertical line or an arrow. It indicates the place at which the next text input of the user will appear.

(Chapter 2)

Cut

Cutting moves the marked text or the marked objects onto the clipboard, from where they can be pasted into other documents or document areas, but also into other program windows. In contrast to copying the original is deleted when cutting.   (Chapter 7 and Appendix 'Getting to grips with Word')

Data field

A data field is the smallest independent unit of a database. One or more data fields make up a data record. An address record, for example, could be made up of the data fields <name>, <first name>, <street>, and <city>.   (Chapter 9)

Data medium

A data medium is a storage medium, for example a diskette or a hard disk, on which you can permanently store your files.   (Chapter 5)

Data record

Consists of data fields (name, first name, street, city, and so on) and is a part of a database such as 'addresses'.   (Chapter 9)

Database

A database is an organised collection of associated data, for example addresses.   (Chapter 9)

Date

The program retrieves the current date from the system clock of your computer or from the date settings of the Windows system control.

(Chapter 8)

Density

The storage density of data on a diskette.   (Chapter 5)

Desktop

The user interface of Windows, on which the windows, icons, and dialog boxes appear.   (Chapter 1)

Dialog boxes

Serve the inputting of data and the selection of commands. Thus, there is a dialogue between you – the user – and Word. (Chapter 2)

Directory

Directories are like the drawers of a cupboard (hard disk). All files which belong together are put into the same drawer (directory). (Chapter 5)

Diskette write protection

Diskettes possess a write protection option. If the small black tab is in the upper position (the 'small window' is open), files can be read from the diskette but it is not possible to write to it.

In this way the data stored on the diskette cannot be accidentally deleted. If you push the switch down, the data can be overwritten. (Chapter 5)

Diskette

These data media can record and permanently store computer data by means of a floppy disk drive. When required, diskettes can be read again by a computer. (Chapter 5)

DOT

In Word file names of document templates end with the comment .dot.

(Chapter 8)

Double-click

The mouse button is pressed twice (short clicks in quick succession).

(Chapter 1)

Download

Transferring of a file or a program from the Internet or a mailbox to your own computer.

Drag & drop

Graphical user surfaces such as Windows offer this procedure, which permits you to move the mouse pointer onto an icon, hold down the mouse button and then drag the icon to a different position. (Chapter 7)

Drop-down list

Only becomes visible when you click on the button with the downward pointing arrow. Then you choose one element from a provided list.

(Chapter 4)

E-mail

Electronically sent messages.

End mark

Indicates the end of a document. (Chapter 2)

Error message

A report from the computer that a certain action cannot be executed or that there is something wrong with the processes that run on your computer.

EU Screen Directive

Minimum standard of security and health conditions.

F1

Function key, which activates the online help of most programs. (Chapter 15)

Field box

A defined area into which data can be entered. (Chapters 8 and 11)

Field box & list

In a field box & list entries can be made independently as well as selected (as in font, and font size). (Chapter 4)

File

Composed of all data (digits, letters, and so on) which are stored under a file name on a data medium (hard disk or diskette). To create files with Word, use the button Save or the commands File/Save or File/Save As. (Chapter 5)

Folder

Hard disks, diskettes and CD-ROMs are often (usually) divided into folders which in turn can contain subfolders.

Windows Explorer and the dialog box of the menu command File/Save show these in form of folder icons.

To save a file in a folder double-click on its icon before you enter the file name and confirm with Save. (Chapter 6)

Footnotes

Notes which are added to a particular text and displayed on the bottom page margin. (Chapter 14)

Form letter

Letters which are identical with regard to most text passages. Only some elements such as the address or the salutation are changed for every recipient.

(Chapter 9)

Formatting template

A sequence of formatting which is linked to a document template under a specific name.

Formatting toolbar

By means of this toolbar 'formatting' is applied. That is you can, for example, choose a different font, highlight text with bold or underline and much more.

(Appendix 'Getting to grips with Word')

Formatting

Determines the appearance (for example bold, italic, font) of text on the screen and the print-out. (Chapter 4)

Freeware

Free software which you do not have to pay to use. Often this licence is limited to private use.

FTP

File Transfer Protocol. A method for the transmission of files via a network.

Full version

A program version without any limitations regarding its use. When you use Shareware you only receive the full version after you have paid a registration fee.

Function keys

Above the writing pad of the keyboard there are the function keys F1 to F12. These do not produce characters on the screen, but trigger a function or a process. What happens when a function key is pressed depends on the current program being used.

Gutter

The Gutter is the additional free space at the inner margin which is needed to bind loose sheets.

Hard disk

The hard disk is (as a rule) a built-in memory device, which permits the storage of large amounts of data even if the computer is switched off.   (Chapter 5)

Hardware

All physical components of the computer.

Headers and footers

Text which is located at the top (the header) or at the bottom (the footer) page margin.   (Chapter 8)

Help

See online help.

Home page

The starting page of a Web site.

HTML

Short for Hypertext Markup Language. All documents for the WWW are tagged with these page formatting codes. Browsers convert these codes and reproduce the documents in their correct formatting on your screen.

Hyphenation

The automatic hyphenation automatically breaks words between syllables or compounds while you are typing.

Icon

Older term for button. An icon is a symbolic on-screen image, which represents a computer function (such as the shape of a diskette for the Save function) or the selection of a control function in the program procedure (for example, a card file box for the opening of a file).   (Chapter 2)

IDE interface

IDE stands for Integrated Drive Electronics.

The IDE interface is the default connection for built-in hard disks, CD-ROM drives, and CD writers. Every modern computer has at least one, most have even two IDE interfaces. Up to two appliances can be connected to each.

Insert mode

Characters which you type are inserted while the remaining text is pushed to the right. The mode is switched on/off with the Insert key.   (Chapter 3)

Interface

Connection between two computer components (such as PC and keyboard) or between two programs.

Internet

Open system. Everybody can access it. Numerous computer systems all around the world are connected with each other.

ISO Standard

Computer work stations must, according to the screen work directive, be ergonomic places of work. This not only concerns hardware such as desk, chair, or computer, but also software, i.e. computer programs. In essence the ISO (9241) demands that software should be easy to learn and easy to handle. To a large extent it should be self-explanatory. Help functions should be designed to support operation of the user interface and the sequence of procedure steps should make sense.

Italic

A script which tilts slightly to the right.   (Chapter 4)

Justify

Text that is justified to the left and the right margins. Spaces between words are variable, so that both at the right and at the left the margins are even. Disadvantage: especially in short lines, ugly-looking spaces may be created in the text.(Chapter 4)

Keyboard shortcut

Holding down one button you operate a second. A keyboard shortcut triggers a certain function. (Chapter 1)

Kilobyte

1,000 Bytes. (To be precise: because computers use a binary system internally one Kilobyte consists of 1,024 Bytes.)

Layout

The allover design of a document. The grouping of individual page components, font, font size, page margins, and so on. (Chapter 6)

Leader

Characters such as dots or lines, which fill the space between individual tabs. (Chapter 12)

Link(s)

Connections (cross-references) to other documents or computers.

Load

To open a document. (Chapter 6)

Look and Feel – User Interface

To put it simply, the user interface is what you can see on the screen. Not only application windows, but also dialog boxes, buttons, and so on are all elements of the user interface. (Chapter 1)

Macro

A sequence of recorded or written commands, which trigger operations and are processed in sequence when called up.

Main memory

See RAM.

Manual page break

To manually insert a page break before the physical end of a page, mark the last line on the page and insert a page break via INSERT/PAGE BREAK.

Via the same menu individual or – if the whole document is selected – all page breaks can be removed.

Megabyte

One million (exactly 1,084,576) bytes. Because of larger memory capacities of the storage media as well as RAM, the megabyte has succeeded the kilobyte as standard unit of size (see Byte).

Memory

A device, in which the computer stores data. The best known is RAM (Random Access Memory). A computer loads program data from the hard disk into the RAM, to be able to run a program. Typical RAM sizes are 16, 32, 64 and often also 128 Mbytes. The DOS memory has a default size of 640 Kbytes (kilobytes) and additionally an extended physical memory. Windows and DOS use memory differently. Windows creates a virtual memory file (Swap file) on the hard disk, with whose help it can work faster, as it can use this area like an added RAM. Normally this memory area is automatically deleted by Windows when shutting down the computer. After a system crash it may happen that the memory area is still present on the hard disk. This is why it is recommended to run a hard disk maintenance program (for example ScanDisk) frequently.

(Chapter 5)

Memory size

The number of bytes (characters), which are available on a hard disk or a diskette for the storage of data or programs. (Chapter 5)

Menu bar

Here you execute commands such as SAVE, PRINT, or EXIT by left-clicking on them with the mouse. (Chapter 1)

Modem

Modulator-Demodulator. Digital data are converted in the MOdulator/ DEmodulator and then can be transmitted via the analogue phone network.

MS

Abbreviation for Microsoft: MS-Word, MS-Excel. (Chapter 1)

Network

A group of computers which are connected via communication links and special network software, so that data and peripherals (for example printer and mass memory) can be shared.

Offline/online

Operating mode, for example, of a printer, a modem, or a network connection. Offline means that there is no connection, and thus data transmission is not possible. Online means that a connection has been established, and data can be transmitted to the printer, to a different computer, or to the network.

Online help

Program functions with which a problem can be solved. (Chapter 16)

Online service

Companies which offer their services, for example Internet providers, via a network connection.

Operating system

Software which enables the computer to work. It controls the keyboard, the hard disk, and the screen displays. Operating systems include DOS, Windows, Mac OS, OS/2 and UNIX.

Option

Changes the settings of Word 2000. Options are usually activated on a tab.

(Chapter 2)

Other formats

All files which are not saved in Word format (i.e. .doc)are referred to as other formats. As a rule these are file formats which are used by other applications.

Data which has been saved in another format must be converted to be able to be used in Word. This is done using conversion filters.

Overwrite mode

Newly typed characters overwrite existing ones. This mode is switched on/off with the [Ins] key. (Chapter 3)

OVR

Abbreviation for overwrite mode. (Chapter 3)

Page number

Consecutive numbering can only be inserted in the header or footer (FILE/PAGE SETUP). (Chapter 14)

Page Preview

Before you print-out a document you should check it in the print preview (File/ Print Preview or the *Print Preview* button). The print preview displays a document exactly as it will look in print. Word literally 'prints out' on screen and uses all available fonts and formatting options the connected printer possesses. (Chapter 5)

Page break

The place in a document where one page ends and the next starts.

Where a page break is in a document depends on the page margins and paper size which are defined with the File/Page Setup menu command.

To insert a page break before the physical end of the page, select the first line of the new page and insert it via Insert/Break.../Page break.

Using the same menu you can also remove individual or – if the whole document is marked – all page breaks. (Chapter 14)

Pagination

See Page number. (Chapter 13)

Paragraph

Continuous text which is felt to be thematically connected and is usually detached by a gap (empty line) from the preceding and following text.

(Chapter 2)

Paragraph mark

In Word paragraphs are created by pressing the Enter key. A paragraph is indicated by a paragraph mark (formatting character, non-printable character). (Chapter 2)

Parallel

A data transmission method in which several bits are simultaneously transferred to an appliance (for example a printer). Parallel data transmission differs from serial data transmission in which bits are transferred individually one after the other (see Serial).

Password

Authentication code for access to the use of software or services. (Chapter 6)

Peripherals

Every external appliance (for example a printer) which is connected to the computer. Strictly speaking, disk and CD-ROM drives are also peripherals, as they are not part of the CPU (Central Processing Unit). (Chapter 5)

Pica

Typographical unit, 1 Pica = 12 Point (usually abbreviated to pt). It is equivalent to approximately 4.2 mm (see Point). (Chapter 4)

Point

Point is an older measuring unit for the size of characters. One Point is equivalent to 0.35 mm font height (see Pica). (Chapter 4)

Port

An interface on the computer, to which peripherals – such as the printer or modems – are connected. A modem is usually connected via a COM port (communications port) which is specified in the operating system. The ports transmit either serial data (normal for modems but also for some printers and other appliances) or parallel data (for almost all printers).

Print

The printing of a document is carried out on a printer installed via Windows. Under Word you specify in advance in the FILE/PRINT dialog box which pages, how many copies, and so on you want to print. (Chapter 5)

Print range

When you print a document – without specifying a print range – Word prints all existing pages.

To print a specific print range you must mark this area and select the FILE/PRINT menu option. (Chapter 5)

Printer driver

A file that contains specific details about one printer or generic group of printers. The computer requires the data to be able to manage the connection to the printer.

Printer types

The most common types are dot-matrix, inkjet, and laser printers.

– Dot-matrix printers

Each character which is printed by a dot-matrix printer consists of a multitude of dots. The dots are transferred onto paper by pins which hit the paper through typewriter ribbon.

– Inkjet printers

Ink is sprayed at high pressure through jets onto paper.

– Laser printers

This printer works similarly to a photocopier. Lasers load individual points on an electrostatic drum, so that it attracts toner. Then the toner is pressed against the paper and fixed by means of heat.

Processor

The CPU (Central Processing Unit) is the microprocessor, which determines the power and speed of the computer. Its performance is expressed by the number of instructions per second (MIPS). An approximate value for the speed of a processor is the work rate which is measured in megahertz.

Properties

Additional information which is stored with a document, for example statistical information about processing time, size, print, memory, and dynamic data, and optional entries such as title, author, keywords, or comments. (Chapter 5)

Proportional script

A script which assigns an individual print width to each character.

RAM

Random Access Memory (see Memory).

Read-only memory

See Memory.

Redo

Click on the *Redo* button to execute a command you have previously cancelled with the *Undo* button. (Appendix 'Getting to grips with Word')

RTF

Abbreviation for the Rich Text Format file format. RTF format is used to exchange data with other programs. It is specified as a file type in the SAVE or SAVE AS... dialog box. (Chapter 5)

Ruler

A measuring device which is visible on the top and the left of the screen.

(Chapter 12)

Screen Directive

See EU Screen Directive.

ScreenTips

Provide information about what the various Word icons stand for. Whenever the mouse pointer rests for longer than a second on a button, a description of the button is displayed. (Chapter 2)

Scroll bar

Part of a document window. To be able to scroll quickly through a document, the scroll bars at the right and bottom screen margin are used.

SCSI

SCSI stands for Small Computer Systems Interface. Appliances such as hard disks, scanners, or CD-ROM drives can be operated via this port. A SCSI interface can manage 7 to 15 appliances.

Serial

A data transmission method. Data is transmitted bit by bit. Modems use serial data transmission.

Server

A connected computer which offers additional services e.g. Internet access.

Setup

The setup of the computer installs essential functions. This specifies the number of hard disks your computer has, what periods are required for certain system procedures, and so on. The setup program should only be used with great care and attention. There are hardly any safety mechanisms against wrong entries, which might crash your computer. You should only change the settings if you know the precise meaning of the individual items.

Shareware

Programs which you may test for a certain period before you purchase them.

Shortcuts

Combinations of keys which call up certain commands. Also links to programs, folders, or files. When you call up the shortcut to Word the program starts as if you had called it up via the Start menu. Shortcuts shorten the processing time in Windows. (Chapter 15)

Sound card

This additional appliance for PCs (hardware) is permanently built into your computer by inserting it into the appropriate board of the computer. A high quality sound card can produce realistic sounds.

Standard toolbar

The buttons on the standard toolbar represent commands which you also can execute with the individual menus.

(Chapter 2 and Appendix 'Getting to grips with Word')

Start-up diskette

A diskette which contains all the start-up commands for your computer. Normally the computer is started from the hard disk. As a backup you should create a start-up diskette, so that you can still start your computer when there are problems with the hard disk, the computer in general, or Windows.

Static data

Data which are changed only rarely or not at all (such as name, place of birth, birthday, or address). (Chapter 9)

Status bar

Here you receive information about, for example, your current location in a document.

Symbol

A small image on the desktop or in an application. It represents a program or a program command.

System crash

Unexpected shutting down of the running program by the computer.

System files

Files which are loaded by the computer at system start-up. They instruct the computer how to use the available memory, where important data are located on the hard disk, and which software and hardware has been configured for it.

System resources

For example, the available main memory and the capacity of the hard disk.

Tab

To design dialog boxes as clearly as possible many are displayed as a kind of card file index, which contains various tabs.   (Chapter 2)

Tab stop

A tabulator (left aligned, right aligned, decimal, centred, and others) on the ruler determines the stop position of the cursor when pressing the Tab key. This key triggers a jump of the cursor.   (Chapter 12)

Tables

In a table text and numbers are placed in rows and columns. The individual boxes which are created by the intersection points are called cells. (Chapter 12)

TCP/IP

Internet transmission protocol which controls the transfer of data from computer to computer on the Internet.

Telephone line

With a modem or an ISDN card you establish a connection between your computer and the online service via a telephone line. For this line normal phone charges are incurred.

Thesaurus

Dictionary of synonyms; Greek for treasure. Here you can find other words with a similar meaning (example: 'building' instead of 'house').   (Chapter 7)

TIFF

Abbreviation for Tagged Image File Format, a graphics format.

Times

Font which belongs to the large Barock-Antiqua group. Times is one of the most widely used fonts. (Chapter 4)

Title bar

Always indicates which document you are currently editing, or with which title (name) you are currently working. (Chapter 5)

Trojan horses

Small programs (such as games) which are offered on the Internet in order to get your password or to transmit a computer virus.

TrueType fonts

Screen and printer fonts which are available in Word. (Chapter 4)

Typography

Theory of designing and applying letters and fonts. (Chapter 4)

Undo

This button undoes the last command you have executed. For each click one more command is undone. (Chapter 7 and Appendix 'Handy tools')

Uninstall

Some program packages contain, apart from the installation program, an additional program, which deletes the files of an installed application. Other programs, for example Excel or Word, permit an uninstallation within the set-up program. (Chapter 16)

Update

Modified and updated version of a program which can be loaded without changing the existing data.

Virus

A computer program which attaches itself to other programs or system files. A virus worms its way into your computer when you are copying files, downloading data or executing a program. Once it is in your computer it carries out unauthorised and often damaging operations.

Web site

General term for pages published on the WWW.

Wildcard characters

Represent characters. That is, they are substituted for parts of a file name, and thus permit the listing of a group of files. The two most common wildcards are '?' for a single character and '*' for an entire or partial file name.

Windows

Graphical user surface, on which commands are executed with mouse clicks in windows and on buttons. (Chapter 1)

Wingdings

TrueType font which is included in the standard version of Windows. It contains a range of arrows and symbols. (Chapter 8 and 12)

Wizard

The Wizards help with the execution of certain steps in Word, and assist the user to solve similarly structured tasks. As in a manual the steps are outlined one by one. (Chapter 8)

WordArt

WordArt is an additional program with which special text effects can be produced. (Chapter 11)

Write-protection recommendation

A write-protection recommendation can be switched off by every user. When you open a document with a write-protection recommendation, you will be asked whether you want to edit it write-protected or not. (Chapter 6)

WWW

World Wide Web.

Zip files

Short name for files which contain other files in compressed form and, for example, have been created with the program PKZIP. Zip files permit a more efficient transmission of data and the space-saving storage of archived data. As a rule you can compress a file to one-fifth of its original size with a program such as PKZIP.

Zoom

The zoom function of Word reduces or magnifies the current screen display of a document.
(Chapter 2)

Index

A

A: drive 73
Accessing documents 82
Activating
– The drawing toolbar 202
– Eraser 240
– Insert mode 325
– Menu bar 15
– Numeric keypad 325
– Options 28
– Overwrite mode 325
– Ruler 242
– Screen Tips 27
– toolbars 24
– WordArt 206
– Write protection 72
Address
– field 131, 168
– list 221
– Addressee 126
Addresses, in form letters 168
– Link to form letters 168
Align
– Horizontal 132

– Page numbers 293
– Tab stops 248
– Text 59
Aligning lines 59
All Clip Art images 192
All
– Cancel formatting 54
– Categories 193
– Clip Art categories 193
– Close 258, 266
– Footnotes 284
– Ignore 43
– Replace 111
– Select 312
Alt key 16, 271, 321
– For starting 10
– Format/Font 52
– Save/Save As 69
Animations 274, 343
Assistant 299
Answers 41, 304
Appearance of
– Button 263
– Cursor 22
– Footnote 282
– Mouse pointer 23
– Table 232, 240
Application windows 340
Arrow 23, 221
– next to line colour 131
– on diskette 70
Assigning 272
– Filename 66
– Keyboard/Command 270
– Keyboard shortcuts 271
– password 88
Assistants 11, 12, 299
– change 300
– choose 12, 300
– hide 12
– in dialog box 302
– switch off 11
AutoComplete 176
AutoCorrect 179
Autoexec.bat 343

AutoFormat 241, 315
– Tables 242
Automatic
– Lists 100
– Names 63
– Size of columns and rows 232
– Tables 240
AutoText 179, 315
AutoValue 282

B

Background
– colour 202, 339
Backspace key 38
Baud 343
Boldface 49, 123, 338
Border 237, 331
– of Clip Art image 194
Border lines 239
– outer 239, 241
Border palette 339
Border types 239
Bottom page margin 120
Browser 343
Bug 344
Buttons 27, 344
– Activating 256
– Adding or removing 256, 333, 335
– Adding to Formatting toolbar 256, 333, 335
– Adding to Standard toolbar 266
– All Categories 193
– Cancel 15
– Center 59
– Close 260
– Copy 332
– Cut 332
– Deactivating 256
– Designing 256, 333
– Document Structure 332
– Draw Table 250
– Drawing 202, 213
– Drawing toolbar 334
– E–mail 331
– Eraser 248

– Font 337
– Format Painter 332
– in the Formatting toolbar 254, 337
– Info 27
– Insert Columns 233
– Insert Microsoft Excel Worksheet 334
– Insert Rows 232
– Insert Table 228, 333
– Insert Hyperlink 333
– Integrating 256, 259, 333
– Italics 50
– Justify 59, 338
– Line Color 212
– More Buttons 256, 339
– New Document 147, 330
– Numbering 338
– Open 82, 83
– Outside Border 339
– Paste 333
– Print 76, 331
– Print Preview 75, 331
– Properties 69
– Removing buttons from toolbar 261
– Repeat 333
– Save 65, 69, 330
– Save As 66
– Shadow 205
– Show/Hide Formatting Characters 335
– Spelling 332
– Start 10
– Switching between header and footer 122
– Text Box 127
– Tips 27
– Tools 87
– Undo 333
Button description 259
Button icon 263, 265
– and Text 263
– Changing 263, 265
– Restoring 264

– Standard 262
Button symbol 263
Byte 344

C

C: drive 85
Cancel 15, 315
CapsLock key 324
Card–file index box 29
Categories Clip Art 195
Cells 228
– Borders 228
– Centering 227
– Framing 239
– Marking in tables 226
Centred 59, 338
Centred cells 227
Centred lines 59
Change
– Assistant 13, 330
– AutoForm 211
– Button icon 263
– Margins 293
– Settings 272, 341
Change AutoShape/Callout 213
Change
– Assistants 13, 300
– Button symbols 263
– Case 315
– Characters 111
– Terms 111
Changing Assistant 13, 335
– Button symbol 263
– Tabulator stop 243
Characters
– Exchanging 111
– Formatting 52
– Inserting 325
– Overwriting 325
– Replacing 112
– Super/subscript 52
– Tabulators 242
Chat 344
Checkbox write protection recommendation 88

Checking document 74
Checking while entering text 44
Choose
– Alignment 81, 97
– Assistant 12, 335
– Background colour 202
– Button symbol 263
– Different colours 339
– Special characters 223
Clearness 222
– in ClipArt 195
– in Tables 222
Clicking an option 28
ClipArt 192, 346
– behind text 200
– Categories 193
– Crosshair 201
– Dragging handles 196
– Edit 194
– Fit 195
– Format 199
– in front of text 196
– Insert 195
– Layout 214
– Move 198
– Outside border 211
– Position 201
– Preview window 194
– Square 199
– via the Internet 193
– Viewfinder 201
– with text in line 198
Clipboard 344
Clips 193
– import 193
– insert via the Drawing toolbar
      202
Clock display 138
Close 258
– Dialog boxes 93, 225
– Documents 258
– Footnote windows 285
– or Close All 266
Colour palette 345
Colour printer 77

Colour
– Area 202
– Font 339
Column
– header 221
– line 234
– number 220
– size 234
– width 234, 236
– inserting 233
– and rows 220, 334
– Marking 229, 230, 233
– Specifying 221
Combination of keys 16
Command range 20
Commands 20, 23, 258, 328
– Change button icon 265
– Close All 266
– Execute 20
– Execute in menus 15
– in the Menu bar 15
– Insert lines 232
– input lines 23
– Undo 104
– via keyboard 315
– via Menu 23
Commands/Keys 272
Common file access 87
Communicating online 354
Computer 345
– Diskette 71
Condition 345
Context menu 26
– Toolbars 25
Copies 75
Copying 103, 332
– Drag & drop 104
– with the mouse 104
Correcting mistakes 39
CPI 345
Creating template 148
Creating form letters 149
Creating
– Footnotes 282
– Tables 220, 333

– Text boxes 129
Creating
– a footnote 282
– a text box 129
– Form letters 149
– Menu items 266
– Menus 266
– Tables 218, 331
– Templates 139
Cursor keys 325
Cursor under text box 133
Customising
– Keyboard shortcuts 270
– Options 274
– ScreenTips 28
– Text boxes 209
Cut 103, 332

D

Data field 346
Data medium 346
Data record 347
Data source 151
– Edit 156
– Merge with form letter 170
– Save 155
Data stored on diskette 82, 330
Data
– for the addressee 133
– Modify 68
– of older versions 73
– on diskette 330
– Store in the computer 70
– Transfer 71
Database 347
Date 135, 136
– Current 135
– Update automatically 135
Date and time 138
Date setting 347
Days of the week 176
Deactivate
– Assistant 11
– Menu bar 329
– Options 28

– Print View 74
– Spelling checker 44
– Toolbars 24
Decimal Tab stop 246
Default tabs 255
Delete 326
Deleting, lists 102
– Documents 90
– Field names 151
– Files 90
– Footnotes 229
– Formatting 57
– Key combinations 273
– Menu items 279
– Read/write–protection 89
– Table line 240
– Table rows 232
– Tabs 249
Desktop 346
– Recycling Bin 95
Details 68
Dialog box 28
Dialog field
– Adjust 260, 270
– Close 93
– Footnote and Endnote 254
– Formatting Graphics 198
– Help 307
– Insert ClipArt 193
– Save 88
– Save as 66, 68
– Tab stops 250
Dialog window 28
Direct help 307
– Switch off 307
Diskette 76, 341
– Drive A: 82, 328
– Size 72
– Storage location 73
– Write protection 72
Document 22, 69, 82, 330
– Access 88
– Check 75
– Delete 92
– Label 64

– Modify 69, 70
– Move 318
– New Names 330
– Open 82
– Open from diskette 82, 330
– Print 75
– Retrieve 82
– Re-use 82
– Save 64, 65, 71, 330
– Structure 332
– Template 65, 66, 331
– Transfer 71
– Wizard 144
DOS 345
Double-click 348
Downloading files 348
Drag & drop 117, 348
Dragging handles 196
Drawing 192, 202, 213
– Tables 239, 334
Drawing toolbar 130, 192, 202, 205
Drive, C: 86
– for diskettes 73
Dropdown list 33

E

E-mail 331
Edit
– Data source 160
– Font attributes 208
– Footnotes 286
– Text box 130
Effects 343
– Scripts 206
– Shadow 205
End 325
– mark notes 325
– of document 22, 348
– of selection 314
Enter
– Numbers 325
– Table text 226
– Text 22
– Text field 128
– Text in Footers 122

– Text in Headers 122
Entries 274
– Documents 86
– Button symbols 265
– under File 86
Entry 23
– Adapt 28
– Format 26
– in Header or Footer 123
– in Print View 75
– in Tables 219
– New 69
– Programs 10
– Save 70
Entry window 28
Envelope 126
– with address window 126
Eraser 240
Excel 334
Exchanging button symbol 263
Execution
– Menu bar 15
– of commands 329
– via Menu 23
Exit 15, 34, 46, 315
– Dialog box 93
– Print View 75
– Program 15
– via icon 16
– without saving 34, 45
– Word 15, 16
Exiting Word 15
Exiting, dialog box 93
– Page Preview 75
– Word 15
Explanation
– at lower page border 283
– buttons 27
– context menu 26
– current command 259
– icons 27
– keyboard shortcut 16
Explanatory text to buttons 264
Expressions, switching 112
– Searching 110

– Toolbars 24
– Unknown 42
Extending search 111

F

Field functions
– Activate 164
– Show 164
Field names 151
– Delete 152
– in data source 151
– Insert in form letters 153
– New 153
– Specify in form letter printing
     160
File 66, 348
– AUTOEXEC.BAT 343
– CONFIG.SYS 345
– Delete 94
File access 90
File format 136
File name extension
– *.doc 143
– *.dot 143
File names 66, 67, 71, 84, 13, 348
– Assigning 65
– Extensions 66
– of document templates 348
– Overwrite 67
File type 139
Files on diskettes 72
– Delete 92
– Information 68
– Save 66
Filing cabinet 65
Fill area 212
– Text field 212
Fill character 250
Fill colour 202, 204
Font 56, 222, 337
colour 339
effect 206, 208
size 56, 231, 337
– selection 317
type 56

Footer and header 122
Footnote 282
– Autonumber 284
– Bottom of page 284
– Complete 286, 288
– Delete 290
– End of document 284
– Endnote 284
– Normal view 282
– Number format 284
– Print layout 282
– Recognise 291
– User–defined 284
– View 291
Form letter, printing 170
– Adding field names 153
– and linking data source 170
– Creating 149
– Field names 15
– in advance 170
– Preview 170
– Saving 171
Format 24
– Bullets and Numbering 100
– Font 55
– Page numbers 293
– Style 53
– Transfer 330
Formatting Pictures 198
– Preview 54
– Remove 58
– Text 26, 49, 337
– Text field 130
– Undo 58
– Using keys 55
Formatting marks 29
– Show/hide 29
Formatting toolbar 50, 337
– Adding buttons 254, 335, 339
– Buttons 27
– Show/hide 29
– via context menu 26
Forms 203
Frame 130, 339
– around Button 266

Framing cells 241
Framing with borders 241
Full Screen View 78
Function keys 4, 325
Function
– Alignment 198
– Close 258
– Dialog fields 28
– Eraser 240
– Form letters 158
– Format painter 114, 332
– Icons 27
– Menus 15
– Options 28
– Remove 270

G
General options 88
Getting started with Word 10
Grammar 44
Gutter 349

H
Handling tabs 29
Hard disk 71, 350
Header and Footer 122
– closing 124
Header lines, on every new page
     225
– Repeating 225
Headings 58
– in tables 221
Height of a text field 131
Help 27, 302, 335
– in dialog box 305
– Symbol 317
Help books 302
Hide
– Assistant 12
– Buttons 258
– Field codes 164
– ScreenTips 27
– Spelling and Grammar 44
– Toolbars 24
Highlighting 50

– with keys 55
Hint 88
– Buttons 27
Home 326
Hyperlink 333

I
Icon 27, 330
– Bold 52
– Center 59
– Copy 101
– Cut 101, 332
– Draw 193, 202
– Fill colour 203
– Insert columns 233
– Insert table 220, 334
– Italic 51
– New 330
– Open 82
– Open document 330
– Paintbrush 114
– Remove 264
– Save 66
– Save as 66
– Tips 27
– If...then...else 165
Importing clips 194
Information on
– Buttons 27
– Commands 306
– Current document 67
– Files 68
– Icons 68
Insert 325
– Characters 325
– Clip Art 192
– Columns 231
– Date and Time 134
– diskette 7
– Endnote 284
– Excel table 334
– Field names 160
– Fields 162
– Footnote 280, 281
– Hyperlink 331

– Mail merge field mode 148
– Shadow 205
– Numbering 101
– Symbol 222
– Tables 220, 334
– Text box 124
– WordArt 206
Internet Chat 344

J

Justify text 59, 60, 338, 351

K

Key combinations 16, 313, 321
– Assigning 272
– Cancelling 273
– Ctrl and Space bar 58
– Current 272
– Deleting 273
– Pressing 272
– Removing 273
– to format 55
Keyboard 2, 326
– Command 272
– Customising 270
– Exiting Word 27
– Shortcuts 315
Keys, third symbol 324
– Assigning to command 272
– Pressing simultaneously 16
Keywords 304

L

Label 64, 328
– Diskettes 72
Landscape format 232
Layout 125, 200
– of a text box 131
– options 53, 194
Left mouse button 6, 15
Left–aligned 59
Left–aligned tabulator 244
Letter Wizards 145
Letters & faxes 141, 145
Line colour 132, 211, 212

Line spacing 256, 320
Line, erasing 240
– between columns 234
– Deleting in tables 250
– Extending 318
– Marking 313
– Vertically 250
Link 333
Linking form letter and data source 172
List field categories 260
Lists 100
– Automatic 102
– Cancel 101
– Insert 102
– Remove 102
– Type 116
Loading 83, 328
Location, storage 65
– of printer 76

M

Mail Merge Helper 148
– Preview 170
– toolbar 160
Main document 146
Margin 336
– Increase 338
– Decrease 338
– notes 284
– of text box 131
Marking
– Beginning 314
– Character 310
– Document 314
– End 314
– Extending 318
– Printing 76, 77
– Rows and columns 229
– Section 312
– Select All 314
– Sentences 312
– Table columns 230
– Table rows 228
– Text 51

– Whole document 314
– Whole text 313
– with the keyboard 52
– with the mouse 52, 310, 312
– words 310
Memory and system commands 343
Menu 15
– Actions 23
– File 86
– Handling 15
– View 25
– Window 92
Menu bar 15, 328
– Deactivating 328
Menu functions 15
Menu item
– Edit 110
– Edit/Find 110
– Edit/Select All 314
– Entry Word 10
– Format/Font 52
– Insert/Picture 192
– Insert/Picture/WordArt 208
– Insert/Symbol 222
– Submenu 10
– Table/AutoFormat 240
– Table/Delete Rows 232
– Table/Headings 221
– Table/Insert Rows 232
– Tools/Language 104
– View 24, 77
Menu items
– Creating 266
– Deleting 269
Menu option 329
– Extras/Customize 258, 261
– File/Close 258
– File/Open 82
– File/Print 76
– File/Save 66
– Paste 264
– Save as 67
– View/Toolbars 25
Merge fields 160

Microsoft Excel worksheet, inserting 334
Modem 353
More, ClipArt 193
– Buttons 256, 335
– Columns 233
– Creating more footnotes 286
Mouse 6
Mouse button, context menu 26
– left 15
– right 26
Mouse pointer 23
– as arrow 23
– as white cross 23
– in table columns 230
– in the worksheet 23
– position 23
– when marking lines 230
– with + 105
Move
– ClipArt 197
– Column line 234
– Graphics 197, 208
– in Tables 221
Moving
– Column line 234, 236
– Drag & drop 104
– with mouse 104

N

Names
– Toolbars 24
– Drives 72
– Documents 328
Navigation keys 5
Netscape Navigator 344
New 261
– Details 70
– Document 46, 141
– Documents 330
– Empty document 140, 330
– Filenames 67
– Inserting field names 153
– Lines 228
– Main document 150

– Pressing keyboard shortcut 282
– Sheet 338
– Worksheet 338
Next column 235
Non-printable character 315
Normal view 123, 124
– Footnote 282
Number format 293
– Footnote 284
Number
– Copies 76
– Documents 86
– Printed pages 76
– Rows and Columns 220, 334
Numbering AutoValue 284
Numbers, entering 325
– with decimals 246
– sorting 248
Numeric keypad 4, 325, 326
NumLock 325, 326

O

Open documents 85
Opening files 82
– Document templates 142
– the Start menu 10
– with File 85
Opening files from diskette 82, 330
Operating system 344
Optical effects 341
– highlighting 337
– script effect 206
Option 28, 86, 274, 340
Options, listing 97
– Designing 192
– for starting 10
– Marking 52
Original specifications 70
Other documents 142
Other toolbars 24
Outlook 10
Overview button 265
– Text wrapping types 198
Overwrite 40, 330
– Activating 325

– Overwriting characters 325
– Overwriting filenames 67

P

Page break 319
Page layout 125, 126
– Footnote 228
Page margin 280
– Changing 296
– Default 292
– Footnotes 282
Page numbers 293
– Inserting 293
– Placing correctly 295
– Viewing 295
Paintbrush button 113
Palette of wizards 12, 300
Paper format 234
Paragraph
– Align 58
– Centre 320
– Format 58
– Justify 320
– Left 320
– Right 320
Password 87, 89
– Confirming 89
– Entering 90
– to remove write-protection 90
Personal buttons 254, 333, 337
Pictures 192
– behind text 198
– Casting shadows 205
– Centre 209
– Crosshair 201
– Fit 198
– Format 198
– in front of text 198
– in line with text 198
– Talking 213
– Move 208
– outside border 211
– Rotate 209
– Wraparound 198
– Square 198

– WordArt 207
Placeholders in form letters 151
Position, on screen 23
– Clip Art 201
– of command 269
– of document 81
– of mouse pointer 23
– of paragraph 338
– of text box 137
– Page numbers 293
– Tabs 250
PowerPoint 10
Print Preview 75, 126, 320, 331
– Exiting 75
– Magnifier 75
Print range 356
Print to File 76
Printed pages 76
Printer 75, 341, 356
– Copies 75
– Drivers 356
– Name 75
– Pages 75
– Range 75
– Type 75
Printing 331
– Preview 75
Printing selected text 75
Printout 75
– Check 75
– Context menu 26
– Document 63, 327
– Form letters 168
– Icon 27
– Redirect to file 75
– Sheet 123
– TrueType fonts 360
Program start-up 10
Properties 67, 357
– Files 67
– Printing 75
– Table 237
Protecting diskettes 71

Q
Questions about Word 305
Quick commands 271

R
RAM 357
Recycle bin 95
Red wavy line 41, 43
Remove
– Buttons 256, 69, 330
– Documents 92
– Field names 150
– Footnotes 290
– Formatting 58
– Icons 266
– Keyboard shortcuts 271
– Lists 100
– Menu entries 269
– Menu items 269
– Read and write protection 88
– Rows in tables 232
– Tab stops 249
– Table lines 240
– Write protection 88
Repeat
– Header lines 225
Repeated phrases 343
Replacing 321
Right mouse button 6, 26
Right–aligned 59
Rotate 209
– WordArt graphics 209
Rows and columns 218, 334
– Aligning 59
– Centred 59
– Deleting from tables 232
– Highlighting 310
– in tables 222, 334
– Inserting 232
– Inserting into tables 242
– Left–aligned 59
– Right–aligned 59
– Specifying 221
– Specifying in tables 230

Ruler, activating 242
– in tables 243

S

Save 64, 66, 328
– Button 67
– Changes 69
– Data source 155, 171
– To diskette 72
– Documents 64
– Extension 66
– F12 71
– Form letters 171
– Saving in 67
Save As 70
– Dialog box 66
Save options 89, 91
Screen 11
ScreenTips 27, 261
– Activating 27
– Deactivating 27
Script 55
– Subscript 55
– Superscript 55
Scroll bars 358
Searching 111
– in 82, 83, 328
– for expressions 111
– for words 111
Security 72
Select
– Assistant 12, 230
– Border lines 241
– Button symbol 265
– Column 233
– Correct word 106
– Row 310
– Sentence 310
– Text wrapping 201
– Whole columns 229
– Whole rows 229
– Whole text 310, 314
– Zoom 33
Selection list
– Font 55

– Font size 56
Sender and Addressee 126
Sending documents via the Internet
    331
Settings 274, 340
– Change 274, 340
– Page 295
Shadow 205
– Effects 205
– Inserting 205
– Play 205
– Type 205
Shapes
– Callout 214
– Drawing 203
– Script 208
– Tables 234
Short term memory 103
Shortcuts 55, 270
– Assigning 270
– Deleting 271
– Formatting 55
– Pressing 270
– Removing 271
Show
– Buttons 258
– Draw toolbars 202
– Field functions 164
– Ruler 242
– ScreenTips 27, 28
– Toolbars 24
Sign language 23
Size
– Automatic of rows and columns
    234
– Clip Art picture 196
– Font 50, 335
– Table column 234
– Text field 131
Small Caps 54, 321
Software 10
– Start-up 10
– Terminating 15
Sorting 237
– Ascending 250

– by numbers 250
– by Words criteria 248
– Descending 250
– First column 210
– in tables 239
– text 238
– values 238
– when printing 75
Space bar 326
Special characters 222
– Selection 223
Special keys 4
Specifications 70
– Addressee 131
– in Print View 75
– in Tables 221
– of Buttons 27
Specifying
– Automatic update 135
– Button 265
– Filename 65
– Footnote 282
– Lists 100
– Number of rows and columns 220
– Pages for printing 75
– Storage location 66
– Table headers 225
Spelling 40, 332
– adding new words 43
– and grammar 44
Standard toolbar 330
– Activating/deactivating 24
– Button 27
– Context menu 26
– Integrating button 268
– through the context menu 26
Start menu 10
Starting 10, 11
– Programs 10
– Thesaurus 106
– WordArt 206
Status lights 4
Status of printer 75
Storage location 65
– Diskette 72

– Specifying 66
Switch off
– Assistant 11
– Direct help 307
Switching between header & footer 124
Switching between windows 92
Symbol 222
– in front of ruler 244
– of button 268
– Word 10
Symbols and arrows 222

T

Tabs 29
– Activating 29
Table header 220, 225
Table, creating 220, 331
– Activating 226
– AutoFormat 241
– Appearance 242
– Drawing 237, 339
– Enlarging 231
– Inserting 220, 33
– Inserting columns 233
– Inserting rows 232
– Inserting symbols 222
– Inserting, undo 221
– Layout 212
– New rows 228
– Pencil 239, 331
– Preferred width 23
– Properties 237
– Ruler 234
– Selecting cells 228
– Selecting columns 228
– Selecting rows 231
– Sorting 237
– with tabulators 242
Tables and Borders 239, 333
Tab stop 242, 245
– Adopting 246
– Alignment 250
– Centred 245
– Decimal 246

- Default 243, 250
- Deleting 249
- Dialog box 250
- Fill character 250
- Left 243, 245
- Moving 247
- Right 246
- Setting 243
- Specifying 250
- Vertical line 250
Task bar 136
Templates 139 – 144
Text
- Changing 68
- Copying 103
- Designing 49
- Formatting of Word 52
- from older versions 74
- Highlighting 49
- in footers 122
- in headers 122
- in pictures 209
- in tables 221
- Moving 104
- on diskette 72
- Opening from diskette 82, 330
- Pasting 104
- Printing 75
- Transferring 72
- Wizards 145
- Wrapping styles 197
Text box 126, 211
- as legend 213
- Clear 212
- Customising 211
- Editing 132, 211
- Formatting 130
- Inserting 211
- Moving 212
- outside border 211
- Transparent 212
Text entry 22
Text headers 58
Text wrapping 199
Thesaurus 106, 319

Tick mark 24
- in front of an entry 256, 336, 340
- in front of an option 28
- in front of default 24
- in front of format 24
Title bar 64, 328
Toggle switch 71
Toggling between documents 94
Toolbar 24
- Activating/deactivating 24
- Context menu 25
- Customising
- Drawing 192, 202
- Tables and Borders 239, 333
- with the context menu 26
- WordArt 207
Top page margin 122
Transparent text boxes 212
Typewriter keypad 13, 322

U

Underlining 52, 337
Undo 105, 330
- Documents 84
- Last command 106
- Undoing commands 106
Undo all formatting 54
Uninstall 361
User interface 11
- Windows 361
User-defined
- Buttons 256, 335, 339
- Files 72
- Menu items 266

V

View 24, 25, 127, 340
- Header and Footer 125
- Document 75
- Normal 123
- Print Loayout 125
- Tick mark 24
- Zoom in/out 75
View Formatting marks 29, 335
Visual characters 29, 335

W

White area 22
Width
– of a column 234
– of a table column 234
– of a text field 131
Window 93
Windows Desktop Recycle Bin 95
Wizards
– Resume 144
– Template 144
Word 10
– Exiting 15, 16
– Exiting without saving 15, 34, 46
Help
– Starting 10
– Structure of 20
– Templates 140
– Updating 135
Word count 104
Word derivations 107
Word meanings 106
Word repetitions 104, 108
WordArt 206, 216
– Designing 216
WordArt object 207
– rotating 209
– shapes 206
– special text effects 206
– toolbar 207
Words, exchanging 112
– Finding 112
– Replacing 112
– Searching 111
– Underlining 49
Working
– in the Assistant 144
– via keyboard 20
– with tabs 29
– with the mouse 20
Write area 22
Writeprotection, diskettes 72

Z

Zoom function 32, 75, 197